CALLED TO CARE

CALLED TO CARE

YOUTH MINISTRY AND THE CHURCH

DOUG STEVENS

Youth Specialties

ZONDERVAN PUBLISHING HOUSE
Grand Rapids, Michigan

CALLED TO CARE
Copyright © 1985 by Youth Specialties, Inc.

Youth Specialties Books are published by Zondervan
Publishing House, 1415 Lake Drive, S.E.,
Grand Rapids, Michigan 49506

Library of Congress Cataloging in Publication Data

Stevens, Doug
   Called to care.
   Bibliography: p.
1. Church work with youth. I. Title.
BV4447.S689 1985   259'.2   85-619
ISBN 0-310-28461-9

Edited by Kin Millen
Designed by Ann Cherryman

Printed in the United States of America

90 91 92 93 94 / DH / 10 9 8 7 6

To the beautiful high school and college-age young people of the Peninsula Covenant Church, Redwood City, California, who taught me everything I know about youth work;

to my students and friends at Barrington College, Rhode Island, who challenged me to sharpen and broaden my concepts of youth ministry;

and to Brandon, Wendy and Diane, my wonderful fast-growing children and lively little discipleship group.

FOREWORD

When Doug Stevens became Minister to Students at Peninsula Covenant Church in Redwood City, California, scores of young people of high-school and college age were involved in the youth program. When he left five years later, there were several hundred. But it was far more than a numbers game for Doug. He had played a key role in helping a settled, middle-aged congregation reach beyond itself to bring Christ to the surrounding community. That the youth ministry has continued to grow since his departure testifies to its being founded on sound biblical principles and not on the charisma of a bright and popular leader.

As I see it, the task of youth ministry is twofold. First, it should lead young people into a growing relationship with Jesus Christ. Second, it should help those young people enter the adult world. The youth worker is not unlike those people in primitive tribes who preside over puberty rites, who guide adolescents through the training and ritual necessary for the passage from childhood to adulthood. So, too, the youth worker guides young people into Christian maturity.

But the task is far more complex than in a primitive tribe. In our pluralistic society, Christian beliefs are openly challenged, and young people struggle with the credibility of the Christian faith and lifestyle. The complexity of modern life has caused education to be extended many years beyond biological maturity, and the struggle lasts through the completion of education and beyond.

To facilitate this maturing process, the church needs well-trained, mature Christian professionals. I believe that all but the smallest churches should have at least one such person on their staffs. The task of organizing a youth ministry is often delegated to an associate pastor or Christian-education director who usually has many other duties as well. Or the task is given to a young man fresh from seminary who simply endures the unruliness of teenagers until he can find a pulpit of his own. Or the position of youth minister is given to a perennial adolescent who has little training and little direction but is able to "have fun with the kids." Since youth workers generally have neither a clear understanding of their task nor vocational training, they are usually put on starvation wages. They are also fair game for any critic in the church who feels that "the young people aren't spiritual enough." They become objects of the hostility of parents who are prepared to make the youth leaders the scapegoats for every teenager's problems, including acne. If the program is successful, then the numbers increase, which, in turn, arouses the ire of parents who feel that their children are being neglected in the crowd. The result is either burn-out or failure, which explains the rapid turnover of youth ministers.

When Doug came to Peninsula Covenant, we both agreed that no significant youth ministry could be developed in less than five years. And five years was what it took.

Another conviction was that one of the most important functions of the youth minister is the training of lay counselors. Since one person cannot work effectively with more than ten or twelve people at a time, he or she will find it necessary to train adults to do much of the work. This does not mean that the youth minister will not also work directly with young people; it does mean modeling the roles of evangelist and discipler for those lay volunteers that are being trained. If this is not done, the youth worker will become the victim of success. He or she will have too many young people to help and reach, and the ministry will eventually grow smaller and less effective. During Doug's years as youth pastor, the number of lay volunteers grew from two to nearly thirty. He modeled well what he taught.

Finally, tension exists as to whether the youth minister should disciple the young people of the church or evangelize the youth of the surrounding community. We believe the issue is a false one. A church that directs its ministry primarily to its own young people has already disobeyed Christ's command to make disciples of all nations. The church that decides to evangelize the community to the neglect of its own people is doomed to failure because only disciples who have been taught to observe all that Christ commanded can effectively carry out the task of evangelism. Evangelism and discipleship are not contrary endeavors. They are both part of the Great Commission and, as such, are the right and left hands of effective ministry.

During the years that Doug was at Redwood City, we became close friends. And that friendship continues. Being outspoken and verbal people, we had many grandiloquent debates on issues small and great. We endured pain and hardship together, but laughter and tears built lasting bonds. He understands youth ministry as few people do. To paraphrase another Paul, "Let me commend to you my son and co-worker, Doug, and his wife, Nancy. Let me further commend to you his epistle, which he has sent to all the churches of this land."

Paul E. Larsen, S.T.D., Pastor
Peninsula Covenant Church
Redwood City, California

11

PREFACE

A standard practice of youth ministers is to piece together a program and then, later, to decide why we are doing what we are doing. If we are fortunate, we may do something right by accident (our good instincts do sometimes save us). But this approach seems backward.

The prevalence of these jerry-built youth programs should be a matter of great concern. Incompetence is not the problem—most youth leaders are, in fact, very capable; nor is there a lack of spirituality. The problem is that most youth ministers are simply operating under a great amount of pressure. When we realize this, we can sympathize with them while still being aware that their hasty and ill-conceived attempts at youth ministry could be so much more effective than they are.

Usually, the pressure the youth worker feels stems from his or her own awareness of the great needs of adolescents; somebody has to do something—and fast. Many kids have big problems, and the horror stories of a generation in trouble have become commonplace. Adults are losing touch with them. Their parents are pleading for help, and the schools don't seem to be holding their interest. The agencies we usually rely on to serve the needs of adolescents don't seem to be reaching as many of them as they used to. Even the churches (when they notice) are desperate. Nothing is working very well, and the reactions to this bleak picture range from indifference to panic.

Then, in response to this potentially tragic state of affairs, a daring and already overextended person steps forward (or is recruited) to start a youth group. The noble undertaking is announced, and a quasi-heroic effort ensues. From then on, it is youth ministry on the run.

After the program is launched and a routine established, one of four scenarios plays itself out:

1. The program never takes hold; the leader becomes frustrated; and the youth ministry, begun with good intentions, withers away after the initial spark of life.

2. The program manages to subsist, but serves only a few youth who prefer the sanctuary of the church to their own native culture.

3. The youth group starts strong and flourishes for a time as a result of some incidental factor such as the charisma of the leader or a surfeit of alluring gimmicks; then it falters and dies— much to the disappointment of those who wished for success.

4. God breaks all the rules and performs a miracle. He intervenes and causes a program to succeed in spite of the failings of the leaders.

The point of this diagnosis is not to demean the sincere Christians who are ministering to youth. The intent, rather, is to provoke us—perhaps even to shame us—into a wholehearted, informed commitment to ministry with young people. It is my opinion that youth ministry is done very poorly in most churches. However, it is also my conviction that any church, whatever its size or denomination or location, can afford, staff, provide resources for, and carry on an effective youth ministry.

Youth are at a crossroads. People who are in touch with kids today have an ominous sense of an accelerating and compounding crisis. Something must be done. There is an urgency about youth ministry, and those who feel it are a giant step ahead of those who assign it a low priority.

By taking this ministry seriously, we are obliged to articulate and apply a philosophy that conscientiously avoids the program-for-program's-sake reflex. All youth programs reflect a philosophy, sometimes without knowing it. Our presuppositions usually bubble up to the surface unexamined, and yet they determine the direction of the youth group. We are in jeopardy of forfeiting our chance for effective involvement when we do not deliberately align our ministry with God's purposes.

For a *philosophy of ministry* to be adequate, it must meet the following criteria:

- Above all, it must be *biblical*. It must be explicitly grounded in Scripture and theologically sound. This implies that we must do more than select a few isolated verses as favorite proof-texts; we must be deeply interested in assembling a truly biblical theology, one that is faithful to the whole of the Bible and cognizant of its central themes.
- Our philosophy must be *relevant*. Historical awareness and theoretical abstraction are not enough. We must find ways of meeting young people in their own environment and responding to them as they are. Our philosophy must be realistic as well as idealistic and vitally related to the personality and culture of our time and place. Youth ministry must be contextualized.
- This philosophy must be *comprehensive*. It must provide sufficient discussion of all the crucial issues and major elements of youth work. All of the tools of the trade should be considered.
- Our philosophy must be *practical*. It must translate into a form that accomplishes what it is supposed to do. We need a philosophy that works when faced with life's real limitations and exigencies.

This is a tall order, but such a philosophy is indispensable. It can be done and is, in fact, being done in many places across the country. The immodest objective of this book is to propose a viable philosophy of youth ministry that seeks to fulfill these criteria and be of use to others who share in this grand and perplexing task.

QUESTIONS

1. Do you think churches today are under pressure to put together an effective youth ministry? Does your church sense the urgency of this?

2. Have you observed any of the four scenarios that may result from the launching of a poorly conceived youth-ministry effort?

3. How do you react to the author's opinion that youth ministry is not done very well in most churches?

4. Do you have a philosophy of ministry? Could you express it clearly in ten to fifteen minutes? Is it important to have such a philosophy?

5. Are you convinced that your youth group's philosophy of youth ministry adequately takes into account the four criteria described in the preface?

PART I

YOUTH MINISTRY: WHAT IT IS

1 A THEOLOGY
OF MINISTRY

THE INCARNATION AS THE MODEL FOR
YOUTH MINISTRY

The philosophy behind any ministry should be thoroughly based in biblical revelation. That means that our understanding and practice of ministry should be carefully modeled on the incarnation (literally, the enfleshment) of Jesus Christ. We recognize Him as Lord and Savior, and we acclaim Him as the preeminent minister. For the Christian, the Son's mission of reconciling the world to the Father is the authoritative paradigm for ministry of any kind (2 Corinthians 5:14–21).

In the person of Christ we receive God's most eloquent self-disclosure. When we accept the salvation offered us in Christ, we are saying yes to the invitation to become like Him, to be remolded into the image of the perfect humanity of Jesus (Ephesians 4:13). In the same way, we should strive to pattern our endeavors after His original, pioneering, pace-setting ministry, graphically demonstrated in the Incarnation (Acts 20:24; 1 Corinthians 11:1; 2 Corinthians 4:11–15). In fact, Jesus Himself establishes this connection.

DOCUMENTATION

To better understand our task, we need to study the ministry of Jesus in depth and in detail. To do this we turn to the Gospels and the Epistles, which portray and elucidate the central event of all history: God's coming into our world. Although my discussion will be cursory, a basic understanding of this material is critical.

This is not an academic study. We are reviewing the New

Testament narratives and subsequent interpretations to distill a theology of ministry. We must interact with the text, ask questions of it, and constantly press toward contemporary application. This kind of Bible study is exhilarating because we have a vital stake in the findings.

We cannot afford to be passive in this living dialogue. Only when we understand the enormous consequences of what we are doing, can we fully devote ourselves to a penetration of the Incarnation and its revolutionary implications. A philosophy of ministry that is not founded on the Incarnation is built on shaky ground. If we do not get it right here, I despair of ever creating a strategy for relationships and programs or of ever being in the place God wants us to be.

The Incarnation is a dangerous subject. The notion that God visited this planet in human form and entered fully into humanity's experience is extremely provocative. It does not suit our religious sensibilities (John 14:8–10). Our sense of propriety dictates that God be sequestered in splendid isolation somewhere beyond the mundane affairs of this planet. We would prefer to ponder reverently a sublime Other who is located in the great beyond. For the sake of decorum, we tell ourselves, we must keep our distance from the holy.

And ever it shall be, except that God decided otherwise. The scandal of the Incarnation is shocking. It is crude. It is undignified. The vague hints in the writings of the obscure Jewish people aroused a degree of anticipation, but apparently even they were confused by the prophecies and largely unprepared for the shattering event.

It is worth reaffirming that the advent of the Messiah is a matter of historical record. The Incarnation is not an ethereal fantasy or a pious tale; it is an event that is historically and geographically fixed (Luke 2:1–4). Even the multitude of references in the four Gospels to seemingly trivial details of time and place and "secular" features reminds us that we are in the middle of life in this world.

But somehow it does not *feel* sacred. It is tempting to dress up the story, to mythologize those features that strike us as earthy and crude (and the church over the centuries has not infrequently succumbed to this temptation). This solemn revisionism has nearly stripped the gospel of its real power. Let us not try to protect ourselves from the truth.

I would like to look at the dimensions of the Incarnation with an eye toward gaining a more complete understanding of the nature of ministry. I cannot think of a more profitable effort for a youth worker.

The Involvement

Jesus did not come halfway to earth, nor did He pretend to be a man (as the early docetic heresy claimed). He became flesh and blood, lived among us (John 1:14), and walked the highways and alleys of first-century Palestine (Matthew 4:23). He was, emphatically, God *with* us (Matthew 1:23), and He was physically present to human senses (1 John 1:1–3).

Jesus was not an extraterrestrial tourist on an excursion, stopping by a quaint corner of the universe to satisfy His curiosity. Rather, He renounced all rights to His divine prerogatives and became one of us (Philippians 2:5–11, the classic exposition of the Incarnation). He demanded no special privileges or exemptions from the less exalted aspects of the human condition (Matthew 26:53–54; 27:27–44).

Although we would expect such divine condescension to assume the trappings of royalty, Jesus was born a Jewish peasant without portfolio into unremarkable circumstances (Luke 2:7; 3:23–38). On the surface there was nothing otherworldly about this Galilean. No one ever complimented Him on the sheen of His halo.

He experienced hunger (Matthew 4:2), thirst, fatigue (John 4:6–8), pain, and death (Hebrews 2:9, 14). He was tempted just as we are (Hebrews 4:15). He submitted, without ever pulling rank, to the rigors of human existence. The humility of God is starkly depicted in Jesus.

At the same time, the full humanity of Jesus does not diminish His identity as the Son of God. It is out of His complete self-assurance that the Son could cross the infinite distance between the inexpressible glory of heaven and the ruinous corruption of earth (Philippians 2). Yet He was not tainted by His involvement, and His integrity remained intact (John 8:46). Only God could undertake such an unrecommended endeavor.

The Appreciation

Beyond simply being here among us, Jesus took a deep personal interest in our lives. He never feigned friendship. Our interests and concerns were His. He was close to people, empathizing with their hurts and joys and aspirations, and He never adopted the typical style of the guru, aloof and distant, dispensing esoteric wisdom from some inaccessible peak.

He actively and naturally participated in the culture of His day. He was thoroughly Jewish, enthusiastically participating in Jewish holidays (Luke 7:34), weddings (John 2:1–11), and other social gatherings. He was immersed in the rural milieu and borrowed heavily from agrarian imagery in His speech. He spoke the language of ordinary people in a way that made an indelible impression (Luke 19:47–48), and there was an immediacy about His physical presence and His conversation.

Above all, Jesus demonstrated authentic love for people (John 11:5; 33–36) and appreciated their true value. He was relentlessly and unhesitatingly committed to people, always viewing relationships as gifts from His Father (John 17:6). There was a bond of fulfilling intimacy between Jesus and those who did not walk away from this supernatural, self-denying love. In turn, Jesus was the recipient of warm expressions of affection, which He graciously accepted (John 12:3–8).

The Secret

As we appraise the celebrated ministry of Jesus, one dimension is easily missed: He kept an astonishingly low profile and was cautious in His approach to His countrymen. He used no razzle-dazzle. He refused to overwhelm others with exhibitions of His extraordinary power (Mark 8:11–12).

For thirty years He lived in relative anonymity. At the beginning of His public ministry, He chose to be baptized. Although John the Baptist, who administered the rite, viewed baptism as a sign of repentance, it was, in Jesus' case, a sign of

His profound identification with sinners (a hallmark of His ministry). This carpenter would not have looked much different from anyone else standing in line by the Jordan (Matthew 3:13–15).

Mark's gospel highlights this incognito ministry. Here we find Jesus forbidding people (Mark 5:43; 7:36) and perspicacious demons (Mark 3:11–12) to publicize His divine credentials. Was He shy or unsure of Himself or deviously using some sort of reverse psychology? These explanations are not consistent with His character. Rather, we can conclude that Jesus was taking time to develop credibility so that people might respond to Him with the right motivation. (John 6:22–59 exposes the dilemma of those who responded for the wrong reasons.)

Jesus did not demand credulity. He never said, "Follow me—just because!" even though, as the Sovereign of the universe, He had the right to extract compliance. Rather, He submitted Himself to be tested. He was patient working with people's doubts, weaknesses, and struggles. He could have compelled obedience in a moment, but that was not His way. He first provided evidence that established sure foundation and then He asked people to put their whole weight on Him.

We must remember that the exodus from Egypt preceded the imperatives of Sinai, which is to say that God displays His love for us even while we are yet His unconscious or avowed enemies (Romans 5:8), and then He claims our allegiance. His stature is not threatened in the least when we misunderstand, ignore, or reject Him and His overtures, although He would have it otherwise (John 12:44–50).

Jesus is willing to win our confidence, although He does it on His terms. He will not perform tricks. But in the midst of messianic rumors, private expectations, and devilish inducements, the One who is to be revealed and endorsed by the Father carefully builds the case for faith. There are risks in taking this circuitous and time-consuming path, but any shortcut to establishing respect for His authority and mission does not lead to the furtherance of the Kingdom of God.

The Healing

Jesus Christ came to forgive, heal, and restore. He was aware of our total need and offered us a total salvation. He responded to our total breakdown with total help (Luke 4:40). He did not carve up people into their physical, emotional, social, and spiritual components, but rather, He was interested in the whole person all at once.

Furthermore, the great compassion of Jesus was not stifled by the attitudes of those He met. He was helpful, even when He received an inappropriate reply. When he healed the ten lepers, only one was thoughtful enough to show his gratitude (Luke 17:11–19). Jesus often reached out to others before there was any indication of how they might react. He did this because He had no ulterior, disingenuous motives. He does not need our congratulations.

The Great Physician is also the supreme instrument for healing broken human relationships (Ephesians 2:13–16), partly because He refused to confirm the traditional friends-and-enemies configurations. He did not accept any prejudicial strictures (Luke 5:27–32; 15:1–2). Jesus was exceptionally versatile in moving recklessly back and forth across social barriers, a habit that, for His enemies, may have been the most aggravating feature of His controversial healing ministry. Any mediator between two warring parties takes huge risks, and Jesus deliberately rushed into difficult situations that were too intimidating for anyone else.

Reconciliation often causes disruption. The powers that be—those who have a vested interest in maintaining division and alienation—would be infuriated (Luke 4:16–30). Jesus carelessly mingled with the poor and the rich, the religious and the profane, the self-righteous and the immoral, the conservatives and the revolutionaries, Samaritans, Romans, Jews, women, and men. Everywhere, He sought to bring healing within each person and between people. His own disciples represented a volatile diversity of backgrounds and dispositions.

The Strategy

Jesus came for the whole world (John 3:15–17), and He never lost sight of His ultimate purpose. But as we read about His activity among the masses, we also realize that He spent even more time with a select few. It was through these appointed disciples that He intended to revive the world (Luke 9:1–6).

Jesus called these disciples to be with Him (Mark 3:14), so that they might learn how to minister to people by listening to and watching their Master at work. Their discipleship was also a lifestyle. He filled them with His life, which they would in turn share with others (Colossians 1:24–29). His investment in them has paid spiritual dividends to the ends of the earth. This principle of teaching and ministering is the key to discipling the nations (Matthew 28:19–20).

But the disciples were not a clique. They came together for the specific purpose of serving others, and those outside this unique band benefited from what was happening to and through the disciples. No secrets were hoarded; no privileges were granted; no lingering in the sweet fellowship of the group was allowed. The entire experience was mission oriented.

The Support

Jesus Himself relied on a variety of sources of strength and support for His ministry. He regularly spent many hours alone with His Father in prayer (Matthew 14:23; Luke 5:16). He asked for the comradeship of close friends (Matthew 26:36–40) even when their faithfulness was suspect (John 16:32). They became a team that undertook specialized functions to reach their goals. He allowed them to contribute to a ministry He could have achieved by Himself. During His earthly stay He was dependent on the Father for anointing and refreshment, and in this way His ministry never became top-heavy with a scurry of activity. His mission was grounded in the divine energy and purpose.

The Motive

Jesus was consumed by his mission; it was His meat and drink (John 4:34). Being in total submission to the will of the Father who had sent Him (John 8:28–30), He had an absolute obedience that sustained Him through periods when the price became exorbitantly high.

Jesus was not simply doing His duty out of a grudging sense of obligation. Rather, He was deeply moved by the plight of those who were suffering (Matthew 20:34; Mark 6:34) and was touched by their sorrows. He was angry in defense of the powerless (John 2:13–17). God's sympathy for humanity is vividly expressed in Jesus.

Just as Jesus never merely went through the motions of service, so, too, He never lapsed into sentimentality about those He served. His love produced action, which is the litmus test of real love (James 2:14–20).

Paul the Apostle also reflects this personal attachment to people. His affection for the Philippians was effusive. When writing to the Thessalonians, he identified his motive for ministry: "We loved you so much that we were delighted to share with you not only the gospel of God but our lives as well, because you had become so dear to us. . . . For what is our hope, our joy . . . ? Is it not you? Indeed, you are our glory and joy" (1 Thessalonians 2:8, 19–20).

Though Jesus was sympathetic toward those He met, His motive for service was not dependent on His current popularity ratings. Even when His best friends deserted Him, when the agony of the Cross stood before Him, and when His desire was to avoid the ordeal ahead, He still obeyed (Luke 22:42)—to the wonder and gratitude of all of us who are the beneficiaries of his grinding endurance.

The Cost

Jesus' ministry cost Him His life (Mark 14:24; 15:31). The pain and suffering he experienced were the price He paid for His full identification with us, but it was a price He had calculated in advance (Matthew 20:17–19). It took tremendous strength, and only the joy of the Resurrection (Hebrews 12:2) and the satisfaction of finishing His mission to a fallen world could have made it all worthwhile.

EXTRAPOLATIONS

What significance does this have for youth ministry? Certainly much more than most of us realize. Christ's ministry is a model that we often fail to follow. In response to the pressure of having to "do something for the kids," we often produce a flurry of programs while remaining only vaguely aware of the biblical pattern and its relevance to our situation.

Even if we do investigate the New Testament model, we may want to suppress the insights we find. Many severe problems, doubts, and anxieties will surface. We discover that it is far easier to manufacture programs that keep the kids busy and off the streets than it is to achieve a truly biblical ministry.

Nevertheless, there is a higher though more difficult calling, which alone qualifies as authentic youth ministry, consciously deriving its sanction and principles from the Incarnation. It is time to focus on some of the inferences that can be drawn from the life of Christ.

The Involvement

Youth ministry cannot be done long-distance. We must enter the world of the adolescent, just as Christ entered ours. We are sent onto their "turf." We must become accessible to them by intentionally placing ourselves in the midst of their subculture (1 Corinthians 5:9–12). In the same way that Jesus moved close enough to touch and be touched, so, too, we are called to minister to youth at close range. It is sobering to remember that the person who is close enough to be touched is also close enough to be vulnerable, hurt, abused, and even crucified.

I learned about this type of involvement several summers ago when I joined a missionary basketball team as a player-coach. One Sunday morning during our tour overseas, we were conducting a worship service at a secluded leprosarium. As I surveyed the congregation from the platform, I noticed the subdued but unmistakable glow on the faces of those suffering believers who were at various stages of disfigurement.

After the service several of the children asked us for our autographs (we were treated like celebrities on this tour), and

27

we gamely obliged. One teenage girl, her scars of leprous deterioration quite visible, approached with pen and pad in hand. I took them, scrupulously avoiding any skin-to-skin contact. I signed my name and a Bible verse and handed the pen back to her, blunt end first.

Instead of taking it she placed her hand on mine, looked intently into my eyes, and said, "No, don't just write your name. Please, write a note to me." My eyes were staring in terror at her withered flesh pressed against my healthy hand. Later, I reflected upon the contrast between my self-conscious attempt to stay clear of contamination and Jesus' selfless and loving accommodation of those who were outwardly unclean and outcast but esteemed in His eyes.

We are called to a passionate involvement with young people, which expresses itself in natural, comfortable ways. As Larry Richards unflinchingly admonishes, we are to "become youth!"[1]

This simple directive to make close contact with young people on their terrain should elicit a definite response from us. Either it sounds exciting or it seems embarrassingly naive and unworkable. How can these things be? By approaching young people in this way, are we making the mistake of taking the incarnation of Jesus out of context? Are we being too literal? It is appropriate to feel these tensions when we are exhorted to literally follow the pattern of Jesus' own ministry (see John 13:12–17, 20).

We must take Jesus' climactic prayer to the Father literally: "My prayer is not that you take them out of the world but that you protect them from the evil one. They are not of the world, even as I am not of it. Sanctify them by the truth; your word is truth. As you sent me into the world, I have sent them into the world" (John 17:15–18). We must realize that He was praying for us. Just as Jesus was sent to us, so He sends us into the world of young people. The force of this directive is inescapable.

In His most famous sermon Jesus reminds His listeners they are to be salt and light in the world (Matthew 5:13–16), that they should become effective in ministering to others. The analogy implies the same kind of incarnational ministry we have been discussing. John Stott has suggested that it is illogical and useless to blame the rotting meat or the darkness for the absence of preservation and illumination. We should, instead, rebuke the salt and light for not being effective.[2] When a sane person walks into a dark room, he does not curse the darkness but wonders where the light switch is and goes to flip it on without delay. The lesson should not be missed. Becky Pippert, in her delightful book, urges Christians to get "out of the salt shaker" and into a moldering world that has a desperate need of the savor of Jesus Christ.[3]

We have Christ living inside us. If we are to be His representatives, we must make contact with people in a direct and intimate way (2 Corinthians 4:5–11). No place is off limits to us, and no individual or category of youth is outside the sphere of our concern. This means we must find them. The youth minister must be willing to go to the campuses, to frequent local hangouts, to visit homes, to attend sporting events and concerts, to go anywhere there is an opportunity to meet with teenagers in natural ways.

Let me anticipate the objections that could be raised:

1. "I don't feel comfortable in those situations."
2. "I don't have time to do this."
3. "The kids wouldn't want me there."
4. "It's an idealized fantasy; it doesn't work."

My responses, for the moment, will be inadequate and abrupt:

1. "That's your problem. Get comfortable."
2. "Make time, or get out of youth ministry."
3. "Yes, they will, if you don't come on as a self-centered, authoritarian adult."
4. "It does work. There are many real-life illustrations. It takes perseverance, courage, and a little savvy."

I am purposely stopping short of specific applications,

which are relative to our settings and personalities anyway. But the principle is nonnegotiable. The process looks like this:

Biblical record ⟡ Implications for youth ministry ⟡ Applications

As we draw close to teenagers (without closing in on or cornering them) and extend our friendship, our adulthood is not compromised. Only mature adults are secure enough to relate to young people this way.

When we understand that our involvement is *for* them, we dramatically change our entire approach. It is not unusual to see the adult leaders of a youth group clustered together during an evening meeting. They sit in chairs while the kids sit on the floor; they sit to the side or at the head table where they can keep the room under surveillance for disciplinary violations; they insist on deference when being addressed; their wardrobe accentuates a foreign culture far removed from adolescent climes; their body language betrays discomfort when they are in close proximity to these "great kids" whose immaturity and bizarre behavior, nevertheless, is distressing; their conversation reflects adult concerns and preferences and, when addressing the younger generation, is couched in an unmistakable parental tone. The result is a semipolite, formal, and strained superior-subordinate relationship that, however mollified by good will, is inferior to the personal, sacrificial involvement demonstrated by Jesus.

The Appreciation

We must be students of youth culture. We must pay attention and listen far more than we normally do. As adults our attitudes have to shift from hostility to mild irritation to tolerance and finally to deep sympathetic interest in and commitment to young people.

When we minister to them in the way that Jesus commands, their concerns become important to us—we make them our own. Our identification with them causes us to take their experience seriously, even when we have questions and doubts in our minds. It is our responsibility to adapt to them and not the reverse. We recognize our shared humanity and search diligently for common ground.

Feelings follow commitments. Love is not primarily a feeling; it is a decision to be *for* someone else. The serendipity of God's love is our startling discovery of joy along the way. As we soberly pledge ourselves to full identification and service, a sense of delight starts to permeate our work, and our appreciation of young people is increased—a by-product, but a highly motivating one.

Several years ago I was assigned to visit a teenager who was convalescing with a badly broken leg. I felt awkward as I walked into his bedroom and explained who I was and why I was there. And as time passed, I felt progressively worse about this contrived situation.

I soon learned that his whole life was cars. I, on the other hand, am singularly inept at anything mechanical, and the area of my brain that controls such skills has long since atrophied. I could not imagine a greater mismatch. I soon fell into an uneasy silence, and left a short time later.

Since I could not refuse to minister to him (I was a lowly intern under orders), I returned for a second visit, prepared to ask questions relating in some form to the distasteful topic of cars. I was reduced to pointing to pictures in his auto magazines and asking, "What is this thing here?" He loved it. The more ignorance I displayed, the more animated he became, and he provided me with excruciatingly minute details.

We became fast friends. At the end of every session, he demanded to know when I was coming back. As my unsupple spirit began to stretch, I learned what it meant to minister to someone in their environment. And I almost developed a flicker of interest in overhead cams.

The Secret

The messianic ministry of Jesus discourages us from relying on our role or rank or from claiming any prestige for ourselves in ministry. Christ's example encourages us to let our humanness be in ample evidence. Ostensibly, our common

31

humanity is never in doubt. But the temptation to resort to titles and other accouterments of dignity is nearly overpowering.[4]

Jesus' method encourages us instead to develop our credibility slowly over time. The Young Life movement refers to this as "earning the right to be heard." We have to prove it, not because we need the affirmation of the kids, but because we are willing to have our love and integrity tested.

To keep the secret requires great confidence. This slow process of loving and serving others without declaration and fanfare creates some ambiguity. We are not making excuses as if we were ashamed of the gospel, but we are taking a risk because of our basic concern that the whole story be known and believed. People deserve better than the hustle and hype of the glib pitchman. If we have to knock them over with "the answer" (or, far worse, with our own impressive position or spirituality), we virtually guarantee an artificial encounter, which short-circuits the possibility of sharing the embodied truth.

In a sense, we need to sneak up on kids. We should not force-feed the Good News to anyone. The Christian faith is easily misunderstood today, and young people are wary of approaching adults. To disarm these fears and to fashion an accurate perception of the gospel is a formidable but necessary task. It is critical that our believability be established as a vehicle for presenting the message of God's love. To prevent a distortion of the gospel, we must be prepared to live out, as well as to speak, the truth over the long haul.

The week I started my youth-ministry position at the Peninsula Covenant Church in Northern California, I volunteered as an assistant varsity football coach at one of the local high schools. Although some people wondered (myself included) if this was a wise use of my time, this opportunity was more than vindicated within a short time.

After I was introduced as "Coach Stevens," most of the team members lapsed into calling me "Doug," and I soon became a fixture on campus with an excuse to hang around. I spent time with these newly acquired friends at games, on the practice field, in the locker room, at the fast-food joints, and at other stops on their circuit. I reveled in these relationships, even though I occasionally agonized over whether there was any real "spiritual" effect.

One afternoon a player took me aside and told me he had to check out a nasty rumor that was circulating. He could hardly bring himself to repeat the scurrilous accusation that I was a "priest." When I confirmed that I was a "youth minister" his face twitched in bewilderment. "All this time I thought you were just another guy," he confessed. "You sure don't look like a priest or act like one. I'll keep it quiet if you want." I held my breath to see if this exposé would affect our easygoing friendship. Providentially, the timing was right and this revelation, with all of our background and history, opened a floodgate of questions about personal and spiritual matters.

Of course, the secret must get out. The mystery of God's redemptive plan is for sharing. Sensitive, prayerful judgment and a knack for pacing will let us know when we have reached the season of openness. As the barriers to faith fall, the attraction of the Savior becomes irresistible.

The Healing

The youth minister should be prepared to respond to the needs of young people at whatever level they are expressed. We should not distinguish between significant and trivial needs. If the person feels it, it is real and deserves our attention.

A young person's receptivity to basic spiritual matters is often a result of the kind of assistance he or she may have received from Christians when there was a specific need—but not always. Offering help with no strings attached will deliver us from the pitfalls of manipulation. We have no need to control others.

Our healing ministry mandates that we be agents of reconciliation. We must be people who develop a capacity to relate to the widest possible spectrum of individuals and groups. If we can move freely among groups and across boundaries, we will exemplify the spirit of the coming Kingdom, which promises to melt all prejudice. Since almost no one does this among teenagers, even the attempt will be a stirring witness. "Why are you here?" is the question in the minds of slightly baffled but intrigued young people who watch the youth minister in action.

The native environment of adolescents is replete with invisible dividing lines. A perceptive look at a secondary-school campus reveals a fairly rigid de facto segregation that is violated at one's own peril. Yet for us to honor the alienation and smoldering resentments would be to contradict the very heart of our mission.

God commands us to invite young people into a new and personal relationship with Him. This invitation includes the opportunity to embrace former strangers, rivals, and enemies. To agitate for change in an entrenched society brings healing and harmony, although some will squirm at the inconvenient disturbance. Someone has to be naive and foolish and bold enough to trespass across the forbidden zones.

Jerry Kaufman is a former heroin addict who is now the flamboyant, irrepressible Jewish pastor of a Puerto Rican and Black church in the desolate Concourse section of the Bronx. As a guest at our college's chapel program, he lectured about the ugly divisions in society and, more repugnantly, within the church.[5] In embarrassing detail he pointed out the symptoms of this sickness. His voice is one of several that stab the conscience of Christians (and youth ministers) who have for so long turned back at the social borders. But if Christ has demolished the borders, we can occupy new territory. We need more emissaries of peace who have renounced allegiance to, and complicity with, the conventional wisdom that advises us to only associate with "our kind of people."

The Strategy

We are called to be completely open with everyone we meet. At the same time, we are called to invest in a chosen few. Many must be considered, but a smaller number will be the focus of special discipleship. For youth ministry, this means that we will need to enlist the aid of other adults to be our co-workers, that we will need to disciple them in the work at hand.

But caution is in order. We must remember that Jesus is unique. *He* is Lord, not us. There is no place for a master-slave relationship between us and those with whom we work. We are all disciples of one Master. But we can live in such a way that our lifestyle will be a model for those who are eager to grow and define their gifts and ministries. They, in turn, will reach out and influence others in an ever-widening circle. This is a deceptively simple formula, which works when tried but is frequently subverted by pressures to maintain showcase programs and their accompanying bureaucracy.

The key to discipleship is spending time with others so that we can become a family, a team, a genuine expression of the body of Christ. Ministering by oneself, with the hope of inspiring or entertaining, is easier and perhaps more glamorous. But in the long run it is always less satisfying and less productive.

We need the help of others. Our strategy is to clarify our goals, cultivate our abilities, and provide mutual support so that we can grow; then ministry can reach beyond ourselves. Individual growth and corporate effectiveness are predicated upon this essential discipleship process. The high priority of discipling adult youth leaders along with the young people themselves cannot be compromised without stunting the progress of the entire enterprise.

The Support

Youth leaders are obliged to give themselves away in ministering to kids, and, therefore, the potential for breaking down, drying up, and burning out should not be underestimated. Only God can accomplish a project of this magnitude. Therefore, we must be constantly receiving nourishment from Him, which means that our Bible study, prayer and sharing times, and other spiritual disciplines must not be a religious routine but experienced as vital, renewing care for the shock troops prone to battle fatigue. The youth group itself will not provide this primary care; the adults in youth ministry must be a part of a nurturing peer fellowship. This is why we have found it important to require every adult leader on our ministry team to be a regular participant in such a group. This tends to keep our purpose and motives anchored in Christ as our needs are being met outside of our relationships with kids. To expect kids to meet our needs will strain the ministry (though they will reciprocate our love, at times, in moving ways).

We need the support of our brothers and sisters on the leadership team who intercede for us and make us better than we could ever possibly be on our own. Both the support system that binds us to each other for ministry objectives and the private devotional pauses that root us in communion with God—both are necessary if we are to have the strength to press on and thrive.

The Motive

Unswerving obedience to God and an endless love for young people keep us in prime shape for youth ministry. These motivations transcend the inhibitions caused by uncertainty, self-doubt, and the vastness of the challenge. When Teresa of Calcutta was asked why she continued to minister to the dispossessed and dying when her ministry could only relieve a small fraction of the misery, she said, "God has not called me to be successful, only to be faithful."

God does not expect us to save the world; there is another, more qualified, and He is the only one adequate for that work. Without any messianic pretensions, we are sent into our corner of the world to be a friend to young people. This limited, though still impossible, assignment becomes our magnificent obsession.

A man once volunteered many hours of his time to help out with a youth program. He told me candidly that he did not care for teenagers (it showed) but that it was the cross that he was called to bear. Christ's compassion, as I see it, never includes contempt or indifference for those served, but entails joy, even in the midst of suffering, for we are constrained by love. It cannot be faked.

The Cost

Youth ministry will cost us our very lives. It will cost us time. It will cost us our dignity. Since we realize that the person who loses his life for Christ's sake will find it (Matthew 16:24–

25), we know that our time could not be better spent, that the dignity we forgo is a delusion, and that the respect we obtain is pure gold. But it will still be hard. The cost is high and should be considered in advance.

Ministry will cost us our lives because God owns us and all we have; He is free to use us and our possessions as He pleases (see Luke 16). I was painfully reminded of this when I casually offered to "pick out something" from my closet for a young indigent who had crossed my path. After my rather magnanimous gesture (so I thought at that moment), I walked into my bedroom and sorted through the hangers, looking for that special thrift-store garment that I would probably never wear again anyway. To my chagrin, my new friend was peering over my shoulder and pointing out a couple of items that appealed to him. Naturally, they were my favorites too and recent acquisitions. There is a yawning disparity between shrugging charity and unstinting generosity, and I realized that, I was holding out on the Lord as well as "one of the least of these."

Youth ministry has been likened to martyrdom, though perhaps that is a bit melodramatic. It cannot be denied, however, that involvement with this age group is intense. The youth minister will have to bring all of his energy, knowledge, and talent to the task and will still need assurance that God will not let him sink.

GRACE AND LAW:
CHOOSING AN ITINERARY

Within the incarnational model for ministry, two opposing themes can be traced throughout Scripture. They are given their definitive form by Paul, and this opposition further explains the character of the Christ-event and its relevance for youth ministry.

The apostle reduces our possible interpretations of God's provision of salvation to two extremes: law and grace. God's Law, rightly discerned, is an expression of His grace, but man has twisted the divine purpose and reinvented the law so that it degenerates into a grotesque mutation. The law orientation

37

seeks to conform scrupulously to external standards to achieve a kind of technical righteousness through sheer human effort. The grace orientation, on the other hand, recognizes our righteousness as an unmerited gift generously supplied by God, which cannot be improved upon but only lived out. (To review the extended Pauline exposition of law and grace, see Romans 3:19–31; 5:1–11; 7–8:17; and Galatians 1:6–10; 2:16; 3:5.)

The conflict between these two incompatible orientations is instructive as we attempt to implement a ministry of the gospel, that is, a ministry that communicates the good news of God's grace. The clash of those two opposing perspectives is exemplified in the following series of head-on collisions:

Freedom versus legalism. It is God's sovereign decision to set us free. The law is frightened of freedom and regularly resorts to rules, codes, censorship, and condemnation to preclude outbreaks of unmanageable freedom.

Love versus fear. Grace is the vehicle of love that is affirming and unreservedly in favor of people. Fear, the law's lackey, is trapped in insecurity and nervously stipulates conditions to safeguard against the unknown and unpredictable.

The spirit versus the letter. Meaning and content are essential for grace to have its impact; the law is enamored of religious jargon and accustomed to clichés and slogans, emphasizing correct form and rote memorization of dogma.

Hope versus cynicism. Grace leans with anticipation into the future and is impelled to take constructive action, while the law is smug, complacent, intellectually dishonest, and uninvolved, never doing more than what is necessary.

Acceptance versus performance. Grace exults in forgiveness and rests in God's acceptance; the law, wracked by eternal insecurity, is constantly driven to demonstrate its own validity and goodness.

Passion versus indifference. Christ demonstrates the depth of feeling and full range of expression that accompanies grace. His life was one of passionate involvement in the lives of other people. In contrast, the dead works of the law produce neutrality and indifference.

Discovery versus restraint. The sincere pursuit of truth is hailed by grace, which touches all of reality; the law pulls back, denounces any shadings of ambiguity, and warns against all unauthorized explorations.

Conviction versus conformity. Grace solicits faith that has internal trust and integrity, while the law drills us in ostentatious pretense and well-rehearsed poses that can pass inspection.

Openness versus foreclosure. Grace advocates that we risk transparency as a prerequisite for sharing and growth, but the law is forever on guard, assuming that all truth is already known and prepackaged in traditional formulas.

Humility versus pride. Grace is not self-aggrandizing but meek. It has no craving for rewards, while the perfectionistic law either beats us down so that we give up, or it incites us to show off our spurious accomplishments.

Inclusiveness versus exclusiveness. Grace transmits to the ends of the earth, overlooking no one, and it is never content until all have been welcomed; the law is a proprietary monument to the pious ones who are busy rating themselves and each other according to the incentives of the game.

Do we dare relate to teenagers guided by the grace orientation? Are we people who have experienced grace to the core of our being so that we dispense grace ungrudgingly? Beyond question, a youth ministry striving to emulate the incarnational pattern will be exceedingly gracious in its constitution and conduct.

This discussion of grace and the implications of the Incarnation for youth ministry needs elaboration. In the following chapters the subjects introduced here will be analyzed in various ways. This chapter of incarnational ministry will continue to guide us and critique our efforts to translate the concepts of ministry into practical form. Without this outline, we would inevitably stray from our course in the material that will follow.

With the concepts of grace and Incarnation firmly in mind, I would like to refine my definition of the word *ministry*. It is not a technical term in the New Testament. It is taken from the Greek *diakonos,* which denotes a table waiter of the servant class, and is applied broadly as the vocation of all Christians. The New Testament uses it almost casually to distinguish those who follow Christ.[6]

The modern tendency to think of *ministry* as the rarified domain of those who are formally ordained is a polarizing and immobilizing practice. It is the responsibility of *every* believer to be educated and deployed for ministry; the Lord is enlisting a cadre of special forces for significant service to young people in this promising era.

QUESTIONS

1. Why is it not sufficient to base a youth ministry on a few theme verses?

2. "A philosophy of ministry that is not founded on the Incarnation is built on shaky ground." Why does the author believe this is so? Do you agree?

3. Why is "the appreciation" so significant to understanding the ministry of Jesus?

4. How are you challenged by the secretive, incognito nature of the ministry of Son of God?

5. Why is healing such a controversial dimension of ministry? Is this aspect of ministry still relevant?

6. Does the strategy practiced by Jesus lead to the creation of elite cliques? Give reasons.

7. Can you remain an adult and still identify with teenagers? How is this accomplished?

8. How can youth leaders avoid breaking down or burning out as a result of their intense involvement in youth ministry?

9. Can a person "fake" youth ministry? What false motivations sometimes drive youth leaders? How are you challenged by the example of Christ?

10. Can you afford to relate to young people according to the "grace orientation" as presented at the end of the chapter? What are the risks? Why is it tempting to abandon a grace emphasis and impose a "law" perspective?

2 ADOLESCENT DEVELOPMENTAL FACTORS

The concept of *adolescence* is a recent one in human history. The term was coined about a hundred years ago to describe a sort of extended childhood that resulted from the affluence spawned by the industrial revolution. Before that technological breakthrough, an individual passed from a quiescent childhood to adult responsibility in one grand leap. At age twelve or thirteen (generally even younger in primitive agrarian societies) the child was ushered into the adult world of full-time employment, with marriage often following shortly thereafter.

The industrial revolution, characterized by the invention of many labor-saving devices, made possible the postponement of adulthood and the prolongation of childhood. That period became known as adolescence. Advanced education was available to many of those whose physical labor was no longer required. Puberty ceased to signify a readiness for a marital commitment. The luxury of more time, during which a young person can slowly ease into adulthood, has become a common feature of the Western world unheard of in preceding centuries. It is now catching on in less-developed countries.

G. Stanley Hall, the acknowledged father of adolescent psychology, viewed these years as a kind of evolutionary recapitulation that humanizes the primal beast. First presented at the turn of the century, his theories seem a bit quaint today. Sigmund Freud (who termed adolescence "a temporary mental illness") and his disciples largely dismiss the significance of the teenage years as merely a reheating of the seething conflicts that boiled during the time of childhood and receded during the prepubescent latency period. It was not until the late sixties and early seventies that a concerted effort was made to study adolescence. Many explanations of the "storm and stress" of this age group were offered and debated. By depicting adolescents more frequently, the popular media encouraged this interest, though society's concern continues to be more apparent at the clinical-research level than in practical application.

Ever since teenagers emerged as an identifiable part of our culture, they have been surrounded by controversy. Adolescents are marginal figures in society. Since they are not children, they no longer receive the support and protection given to the more compliant and cuddly youngsters. And since they are not adults, they cannot yet claim the privileges of adulthood. Adolescents are caught between two periods of life; being neither dependent children nor autonomous adults, they are aware that both groups are given more respect, security, and necessary resources than they are.

To make this transition even more difficult, our culture offers no formal rite of passage into or out of adolescence. There is a complex of events that vaguely resembles such a rite, but it is seldom straightforward. Since America is a civilization in which status is achieved, for the most part, and not conferred, the place of teenagers is highly ambiguous.

Bar mitzvahs, confirmations, entrance into middle school, even the purchase of a girl's first bra are some of the outward signs that childhood is over. As subtle as these entrance rites are, the exit rites are even more problematic, and their symbols are only conjectural. Full-time employment, graduation from high school or college, marriage, the right to vote, turning twenty-one, having children, and owning a car or a home in combination with other evidences of accomplishment may grant an individual passage into a probationary adulthood.

To complicate matters further, many adults do not relate well to adolescents. At best they are uneasy, expressing their concern with a furrowed brow and a glum sigh. At worst they are at odds.

The following extract satirizes this intergenerational hostility:

> So I was sitting in this restaurant, trying to eat, but it wasn't working. I was having digestive problems, see, because of what was behind me. Teenagers, that's what— loud ones with greasy hair. Bad complexions, too.
>
> Anyway, the girls, they were giggling at anything the guys said, even though the guys were saying dumb things. And when they weren't giggling, they were snapping gum. Ever see someone snap gum and eat food at the same time? Teenage girls do it all the time. They were eating pizza, by the way. I didn't even know the restaurant served it, but I should have, because that's all teenagers eat—pizza. With the works, double-thick crust and extra cheese. Most of the cheese ended up on their chins and, of course, being teenagers, they didn't wipe it off. Digestive problems, that's what they gave me.
>
> I'm bringing this up because things have gotten out of hand. Everybody knows that teenagers are low forms of vegetable life. Maybe it's not their fault; science has shown they all have hormonal imbalances. The point is they've been allowed to run around unregulated for too long. I am not the only one who thinks so.
>
> For starters I say we ban teenagers from movie theaters. A month ago I went to this movie, right? It was supposed to be good, but I couldn't enjoy it because of what was in front of me. Teenagers, that's what. Loud ones. The girls, thinking they were cute kept switching seats. The guys kept cupping their hands and making bird sounds, which sent the girls into giggles, their IQs obviously being lower than their ages. This has to be stopped. From now on, no more teens at the movies.
>
> Ban them from congregating in public, too. It should be a felony for more than two teenagers to congregate within 100 yards of any adult. Put one teenager alone in public and you have no problems. A teenager alone is embarrassed just to be alive. Put two or more together and they start smoking cigarettes, snapping gum, lighting matches, stepping on ketchup packages, tripping each other, making obscene gestures and breaking pencils on their heads. Visual pollution, that's what they are.

45

They are also capable of noise pollution. Teenagers do not know how to talk. None of them. When they try, it sounds like they are on drugs.

"Hey, ya hear about the QUEEN concert? Solid, man, I mean, way solid. Like, why don't we go for it, you know? Waddaya mean, ya can't? Don't be such a wicked awesome skeebo sleaze. I mean, really. Come on, don't be a royal wimpout."

Maybe you can't blame them. Science has shown that teenagers' brains are 80 percent unformed broccoli. Still, whoever's fault it is, endless dronings on questionable music and sexual frustration cannot be tolerated. For society's sake, I say we ban them from saying anything at all.[1]

This caricature is hardly sympathetic, but it is one that, with some variations, many of us subscribe to. Why do adults have such a hard time getting along with adolescents? I believe there are several reasons for this antagonism. Let me temporarily adopt the jaundiced view of the slightly contemptuous adult and list a few:

1. *Teenagers are awkward.* They are physically developing, and everything does not yet work with precision. Furthermore, they have not cultivated the manners and finesse of their elders. They stumble and blurt and giggle and belch.

2. *Teenagers are pseudosophisticated.* They try to act like adults, but they fail miserably. Their attempts to affect worldliness are inept and outlandish. They almost look like adults, but they fall far short of adult expectations.

3. *Teenagers are trying to barge into the adult world.* There is a need to limit their mobility to preserve adult sanctuaries.

4. *Teenagers do not show respect for adults.* Young people are not properly thankful for what the older generation has achieved and many times do not concede their right to call the shots.

5. *Adults are sometimes (secretly) envious of teenagers.* They are unwrinkled, healthy, vibrant, and not yet jaded by the realities of the world. The commercial emphasis on youthfulness doesn't help lessen adult envy either.

6. *Adults who have never resolved their own private adolescent crises project that distress on this generation.* They prefer to avoid any reminder of the way it was.

Most adults simply do not like to be in the company of adolescents for at least some of these reasons. To be outnumbered by them is even more unpleasant; to empathize with them is nearly impossible. Adults have enough problems of their own without being flushed out from behind their own barricades into an alien culture. For a meaningful and mutually enjoyable encounter to occur, it takes an extraordinary effort on both sides.

Before an adult can make a positive difference in the life of a young person, he or she must first make an attitude check and brush up on the many facets of adolescent development. Although the following summary is only a brief outline of the pertinent factors, it highlights some of the salient characteristics of this process as described by several leading theorists.

THE FAMILY

The family is the child's universe. Its influence is critical in shaping the personality and affirming the worth of the child at an early age. But as the child approaches adolescence, this frame of reference begins to change. With greater mobility and sharper powers of analysis, the adolescent realizes that the world is a bigger and much more complicated place than he or she ever believed. Mom and Dad are no longer infallible and omnipotent. These former heroes are revealed to be mere humans and are gradually replaced by a new pantheon of pop idols.

At this point, the peer group begins to exert more influence as the teenager spends a greater amount of time with friends. To be accepted by them is now of paramount importance. This experience with peers is the bridge to adulthood, while the family, as a vestige of childhood, is being unceremoniously shed.

Parents, however, remain surprisingly significant people to their children throughout these years. Parents are taken for granted much of the time and even ignored, but they are sorely missed if they are absent. Ideally, they provide a secure home base from which the adolescent can venture into the inviting though fluctuating world of peers. The trips home may become less frequent and shorter as new attachments and outposts are established. For better or worse, the day of full emancipation draws closer.

Virtually all parents feel some tension during this period. The safety net of childhood is gone, and the risks become more alarming (in fact, since not everyone survives adolescence, the worries of parents are not entirely unfounded). But ready or not, the adolescent's urge to break away is increasingly insistent, and parents are wise to prepare for it and actively facilitate it by pacing their own abdication of power as they encourage the adolescent to assume greater control.

Youth ministers must recognize that many parents will not be able to cope with their children's adolescence. The family that, for whatever reason, cannot supply the requisite love, character training, and nurture will bequeath an emotional deficit to their children. The youth worker must be aware of the very serious problems that can occur.

The story of Lisa, a sixteen-year-old who had never really had a family, is a distressing illustration:

> The little girls had had enough. For years their stepfather would stumble into their bedroom stinking of beer and growling at them to move over. He was a small man with a greasy ducktail and a pockmarked, unshaven face that prickled their skin.
>
> He wore T-shirts with yellow sweat stains and cowboy boots with pointed toes. He had served time in prison for assault and liked to slap the girls and kick them with his boots. He swore he would cut their throats if they ever told what he did to them.
>
> Lisa's sister was nine. Lisa was eight. They knew what he did to them was wrong. It was dirty. It hurt. But they didn't dare tell anybody. There was only one way to stop it, they decided. Kill him. They were in their pajamas. The older sister clutched a steak knife she had taken from the kitchen.

Lisa trailed behind. Their little bodies shook as they walked along the corridor. But they kept going. They knew no one else would help.

They walked into his bedroom. The sister with the steak knife. Lisa on tiptoe. They could hear his heavy breathing. But he wasn't sleeping. As they got nearer, he sat up, his eyes on fire. "So you want to kill me, eh?" he sneered. "Come on, try it." The girls shrieked and ran from the room.

Months later Lisa and her sister got the courage to tell their social worker. The state had been involved with the family since Lisa was two because of reports that she and her sister were neglected and abused. Lisa's mother, a "speed freak," admitted she was frustrated about raising children and asked the state for help. Later she changed her mind. There was no proof of criminal wrongdoing but the girls were taken from their home this time and Lisa, confused and unsettled, couldn't make it in a foster home and ended up at a state center for children.

Few of the youngsters went to school. Few obeyed rules. They smoked marijuana in their rooms. Lisa remembers drinking beer, Southern Comfort, and rum. Every day there were fights and the kids carved an elaborate and inviolable pecking order. Lisa listened to their talk about being cool. About breaking into homes and stealing. Shoplifting. Joyriding in stolen cars. Running away. Sex.

Her mother never wrote, never called, never visited. Lisa felt discarded. In a diary she wrote when she got older, she reflected: "I began thinking of myself as being hatched—not born. I was punished for something that wasn't even my fault. I hated my parents. I hated my life. There was no room for love."

To survive, Lisa became like them. She started chiseling her own niche by throwing a clothes iron at a girl who was teasing her. She beat up another girl. "I ain't taking no more s—," she exclaimed. She was ten.

Lisa was transferred to a training school where she noticed Chris, a street kid from the slums who had been in constant trouble since he was nine. Lisa liked the way Chris talked—fast and cool. She ran from a group home to be with him.

It took less than a day for Chris to pop the question. He didn't want to live with a woman who didn't offer respect,

49

he explained. On that particular street that meant she had to get him money. She had to go on the streets, he said, and be his hooker. "Peer pressure was overpowering," Lisa wrote four years later. "I found that I had to toughen up, follow the crowd, be cool." She said yes.

Standing on the street corner, Lisa had smeared her face with eye makeup and rouge and dressed up in high heels and a long dress. It was her first night. She was so scared she pumped herself up on drugs and gin.

It didn't take long before a man in his mid-30's stopped his car near the gutter where Lisa was standing. "Wanna date?" she asked. She had practiced the line for hours, it seemed, trying different inflections that might make her sound older. She was 12. She took him to a parking lot. It was over in minutes. She was $15 richer. Chris was thrilled.

Within months Lisa was making $200 to $300 a night. It was easy. But she didn't like it. Sometimes she would yell at Chris. "I quit. I don't wanna do it anymore." But Chris would calm her down. He didn't believe she really wanted to quit. "Okay, okay," he recalls telling her. "It's her act to make me feel like she's doing it for me, so I just play along with it."

Lisa tried to get a real job. But everyone said that at 13 she was too young. She didn't have enough "experience." She bugged Chris to get an apartment. She talked about the future, getting a real job, starting a family. But Chris didn't care about those things. He was shooting cocaine into his veins, high in street heaven with dollar bills stuffed into his pockets.

Once, when Lisa was in jail, Chris recruited another hooker. Lisa was angry and jealous. She wrote a letter to him telling him to get lost. "I loved him," Lisa recalls. "But I don't think he loved me. What he loved was money." Chris, secure with his new partner, was philosophical. "Once a whore always a whore," he said. "She'll come back. She always has."

Lisa returned to the training school, which was boring but stabilizing. She had few thoughts of religion, but decided to receive her first communion. The confirming bishop told the delinquents, who looked innocent in neat suits and dresses, that they should thank Lisa for making the banner that hung outside the chapel. Lisa's banner read: "We Are The New Creation."

Parents smiled and hugged their kids. Lisa read a passage during the ceremony. But no one came to see her. She didn't expect her mother to come. But she was disappointed that she didn't. She wanted to show her how well she was doing. Lisa was led from the confirmation in handcuffs.

Lisa tried hard to get her act together. Her anger toward the system was subsiding. Even she was surprised at how she was mellowing. A judge released her to a new foster home, and she began to take school seriously.

Then the word came through an uncle that her mother was dead. She had killed herself at the age of 34. Lisa didn't know how to feel. At the wake in front of the casket her stepfather came over and said he wanted to talk to her. They went outside and smoked. "I know what I did to you a long time ago was sick," he began. "*What* was sick?" Lisa asked as she looked away. They stood in silence. "I'm still the same as I was," the stepfather finally said. Lisa replied: "I've gotten a whole lot worse."

Lisa didn't talk about her mother's death. She began skipping school again. With her mother dead—even though she had been little more than a symbol of what life could have been—Lisa felt terribly alone. There was no reason to shine now. A few weeks after her mother's death Lisa ran away. She told a friend that she had been having nightmares about her stepfather, and her mother.

She left behind a dozen snapshots of her mother spread on top of her dresser. They were happy pictures. Family pictures. Christmas. Thanksgiving. Her mother, bleached blond, smoking cigarettes. Her stepfather holding Lisa on his lap. Nearby was a notebook she used at school. It was marked with scribblings and doodles. One message stood out. Over and over she wrote—maybe 150 times—her dead mother's name.[2]

There are too many girls and boys like Lisa who have never had parents who cared and in whom they could put their trust. A variation of this same heart-wrenching story is given in an article about a subtle form of child abuse practiced by "decent" parents.

We hear and read a lot about parents who knock their children around, starve them, force them to live in filth or otherwise abuse them physically or emotionally. It is in vogue to think of such parental abuse taking place in shacks and ghetto apartments, perpetrated by people of few resources and dim intelligence. Poor people, dumb people, rotten, mean, selfish, stupid, scared people who don't know anything about anything. Sometimes that is true.

Sometimes, however, the very models of middle- or upper-class respectability exhibit identical behavior. More often these privileged abusers use more subtle means. They simply withhold themselves and their love from their child.

It is a killer. It is slow and it leaves no bruises. It's hard to spot since the schools, clothes, summer camps and other trimmings seem to be evidence of parental love.

I knew of one such kid who had his own new car and private apartment in the family manse by age 16. He had been everywhere and done just about everything. His parents went their way and he went his in a very well-mannered cadence. He jumped off a water tower to his death at age 17.

I knew another one who told me once about his most memorable Christmas. He was about 10 years old and came home on a train from a private boarding school in the east. He was met at the station by the family car and driver. At home there was a note from "Mumsey." It said she and "Daddy" had gone to the Bahamas for the holiday to escape the terrible winter. There would not be time for him to join them. But never mind. His presents were in a closet. He was to ask the cook for anything at all he wanted for Christmas dinner and, if he chose, the driver would take him around to see all his chums on Christmas day. Love, love, love, Mumsey.

The victim of this velvet abuse was 33 years old when he told me about it. He wept. (He had become very much the same kind of invisible parent, by the way.)

People who cannot hug and snuggle and enjoy time spent with children are well advised not to conceive and bear them. Kids aren't decorative accents or historic testaments to the normal sexual functioning of their parents. They are much more than that. You cannot produce decent human beings without having a rollicking good time with them now and then, and providing them with lots of strokes, pats, smooches, conversation and smiles in between times. You most certainly cannot pay to have all this done.[3]

I believe that every family, no matter how healthy and spiritually attuned, can benefit from having other adults befriend their children, especially during the teenage years. Interested adults can provide relief from an overheated home atmosphere, outside of the rumblings of the authority structure. Nevertheless, parents are still the most important adults in the lives of adolescents. Outside assistance cannot completely replace family relationships.

PHYSICAL DEVELOPMENT

Puberty, that implosion of mischievous hormones, alters the human body with a violence second only to the trauma that takes place during the first two years of life. Although infants lack the self-awareness to reflect on their metamorphosis, adolescents are able to ponder their predicament with great anxiety.

The growth spurt, the change in body shape, the appearance of secondary sexual characteristics, and the development of the reproductive system, all demand great emotional resources and the ability to adjust. The changes can be sudden or drawn out over many years, but their effects are deeply felt.

On the average, girls precede boys in physical development by about two years. In early adolescence (ages twelve to fourteen) girls are generally heavier and taller, and their rounder figures, caused by the increased body fat, contrast with the more muscular (especially upper-body) angularity of boys.

This maturity gap has social implications. For cultural as well as physiological reasons, adolescent girls seem to be far ahead of their male peers in emotional maturity. They are often more expressive of feelings and more responsive to the interests and needs of others. It has been noted that girls enjoy association with other girls for the sake of personal friendship, while boys tend to congregate around common interests, with the personal dimension in the background.

Few people are "average" as they run the gauntlet of physical growth. To be noticeable in any way (or even to imagine oneself as unusual) exacts a high price on an adolescent's feelings of acceptance.

For early adolescent boys to excel in athletic activities is still a mark of prestige. The boy who attains a manly stature and physique before his friends is usually at an advantage if he can perform at a level commensurate with his appearance. If not, unrealistic expectations may press him to retreat. The more slowly developing boy is generally at a disadvantage and must cope with a temporarily stifled potential and more limited opportunities.

The precocious adolescent girl is most likely to be the object of both admiration and puerile jibes. Even positive attention, especially if it originates from older males on the prowl, may create its own problems. The latedeveloping girl may feel left out and wonder if nature will ever begin to stir within her boyish form.

This challenges us in youth ministry to be sensitive and discrete and accepting of the wide spectrum of physical development represented in any group. The youth leader who inadvertently gravitates toward the more attractive and well-endowed may provoke jealousy and resentment, and he or she may miss opportunities to affirm those who need it most.

Many of the weight-related problems that occur in adolescence, such as obesity and anorexia nervosa (self-imposed starvation), require therapeutic attention. Obesity from overeating often indicates that food is being used as a pleasure-giving substitute for affection. The anorectic is often morbidly self-denying in reaction to well-meaning but overcontrolling parents. Normal body functions are disrupted, affecting menstruation (the majority of those afflicted by weight problems in our figure-conscious society are girls), mood, and good judgment.

INTELLECTUAL DEVELOPMENT

The work of the late Jean Piaget is the starting point for modern child developmental psychology. In his extensive research he identified four stages of human intellectual development. The first two stages are usually completed in early childhood. The third stage, the ability to perform logical operations, is achieved by age seven and permits the child to classify objects by their similarities and differences. The fourth stage may be reached by age twelve and signifies a breakthrough into abstract, experimental thought.

Further investigation has detected that many people do not reach this fourth level of mental sophistication or that they only make use of this mode of thought in certain settings. The key factor in being able to think abstractly is the presence of environmental stimuli. Otherwise, apart from such prodding and practice, the capacity may remain unrealized.[4]

The church should take seriously this newly acquired aptitude for contemplative and abstract thought in young teenagers while at the same time recognizing the need for concrete illustrations. Neither hypothetical abstractions nor isolated examples are sufficient by themselves. The adolescent mind can be stretched and stimulated by the youth minister whose approach is elastic.

EGO DEVELOPMENT

The peer orientation of adolescents has been the subject of interest, consternation, and haggard cliché. Extrication from the nuclear family is underway, and in the tug of war for loyalty their power of endorsement gives the peer group greater pull. For adolescents, their relationships with parents, however harmonious they may be, are reminders that they are still children. Reaching toward a future that goes far beyond the limitations of childhood is, by this time in life, a fundamental exercise.

Erik Erikson, a renegade among the orthodox Freudians, provides a framework for assessing this struggle. In his scheme of normative development, Erikson alleges that the adolescent must negotiate a formidable identity crisis. This comes after the development of a sense of competence and achievement in childhood and sets up the crisis of intimacy for the young adult.

According to Erikson, a firm sense of identity includes a perception of one's uniqueness, a perceived continuity of

55

experience, and solidarity with ideals. This identity involves a commitment to a sexual orientation, a primitive ideological stance, and a focused vocational direction. Yet this process of self-definition is also one of negation as much as it is one of affirmation. The trick is to negate the known and to affirm what is only partially known, to risk leaving the given and the familiar, and to leap into an uncertain future. The final product is a well-developed identity that is also a flexible unit. The successful attainment of Piaget's four stages of intellectual development is a prerequisite for achieving Erikson's ego identity.[5]

The greatest change in an adolescent's self-concept occurs between the ages of twelve and fifteen. Early adolescents attempt to consolidate the lore of their family, their childhood experiences, and the oscillating feedback of their companions into a coherent, realistic, and certifying image they can live with and build on. It is no wonder that these years can be exceptionally traumatic and perplexing. One scholarly observer has moaned, "It is unclear where to draw the line between normal adolescent development and pathology."

For the purposes of youth ministry, this research has a relevant application. The youth worker should be alerted to the probability that early adolescents (junior-high age) will be in the process of settling the issue of masculine versus feminine gender identity; that middle adolescents (senior-high age) will be constructing a primitive philosophy of life; and that late adolescents (college age) will be selecting from a narrowing array of vocational options. These constituent themes of the adolescent identity crisis can resurface in subsequent identity tremors.

Inspired by the work of Erikson, James Marcia expanded upon the notion of the identity crisis. He devised an identity status pattern that specifies four "places" a person can be with regard to the challenge of identity formation. This analysis offers helpful insights to youth workers. The four "places" are as follows:

Identity Achieved. The individual has wrestled with the

alternatives and made a personal commitment to an integrated identity. This may require time and may not be fully accomplished until the adolescent moves away from home. High identity achievement, not coincidentally, is usually rewarded in males but often incurs some penalties for females who are encumbered with traditionally restrictive roles (although females, in general, prove more adept at achieving intimacy). Marcia discovered that although girls start out in adolescence ahead of boys, they take longer to achieve an adult identity (a girl's positive identification with an independent mother seems to help). Finally, high-identity status is often the result of less parental control, more praise, and growing up with a "masculine" father.

Identity Moratorium. This person is in the midst of weighing and actively struggling with the alternatives in anticipation of making binding decisions. He or she can be volatile and somewhat insecure but is probably on the necessary pathway to an independent identity. This person desires encouragement and space to maneuver. Marcia notes that moratorium types experience an ambivalent disengagement from their mothers.

Identity Foreclosure. A person in this state will often be mistaken for an identity achiever. Because they are well-behaved and submissive to authority, they usually create no disturbance—unlike the moratorium type. But the foreclosed individual has never grappled with the issues of identity; they have simply accepted the identity attributed to them. Foreclosure types tend to have active, coercive fathers.

Identity Diffusion. This person is wary of struggle; the quest for selfhood has been stymied in the past. He or she has no real sense of identity, and tends to be confused, withdrawn, feeling uncomfortable and out of place. Fantasy and flight are the tactics of retreat preferred by this type. These dejected individuals have inactive fathers.[6]

It would be instructive to evaluate the attitude of the church in relation to this identity pattern. To be succinct, it is my observation that we both admire and fear the identity achievers (unless we can domesticate them); we grow critical and impatient with the moratorium types; we bless the compliant who exhibit foreclosure behavior; and we condemn or pity the diffused "losers."

MORAL DEVELOPMENT

Indebted to the efforts of Piaget, Lawrence Kohlberg, another student of cognitive development, has formulated a scheme of progressive moral development. This approach has generated enthusiasm among educators who recognize that the ethical dimension has been a missing component. Inadvertently, the radical relativity of the values clarification method is partly responsible for this vacuum of moral presuppositions. Kohlberg's work was been diligently followed by many in ministry with youth.

Kohlberg postulates that we move through three levels of moral development, which are subdivided into stages. The first, a preconventional level divided into two stages, is characterized by a childish preoccupation with the hedonistic consequences of behavior. Most adolescents, he has found, are at the second level, where behavior is motivated by conformity to social expectations. Elements of this second level are found in stages three and four, which differentiate ascending steps of moral reasoning. At stage three the person views "good" behavior as that which is approved by others. At stage four the person adopts a "law and order" orientation that credits a designated authority as the final arbiter of morality. In level two the unmitigated selfishness of level one is superseded by a mindset that is responsive to the wishes and guidelines set by others.

The third level, which is postconventional autonomous, recognizes that the convictions of conscience have validity apart from any reward from authority figures. At this level, morality is not a utilitarian concept but is allied with an impartial social contract (stage five) or a universal ethical principle (stage six). Kohlberg has speculated about a hypothetical stage seven, which is based on the biographies of great spiritual figures.

Kohlberg made the following conclusions: (1) Moral development invariably takes place in succeeding stages; (2) one cannot comprehend reasoning at a stage that is more than one stage beyond one's present stage; (3) one is cognitively attracted to reasoning that is one stage beyond one's present stage; and (4) upward movement is effected when *cognitive disequilibrium* is introduced. *Cognitive disequilibrium* is a state of anxiety that occurs when a person cannot solve a problem by means of their current moral understanding; they feel inadequate in the face of this new dilemma.

Kohlberg further states that productive moral discussion is fostered by (1) exposure to the next higher stage of moral reasoning; (2) exposure to situations raising problems and contradictions in such a way that dissatisfaction results; and (3) an atmosphere of dialogue and free exchange where open comparison of possible solutions can take place.[7]

The practice of youth ministry is challenged by this body of theory, but not because it is unfriendly to the Christian faith. Instead, it is our methodology that is suspect. Often we are afraid of any disequilibrium and try to head it off or smooth it over before anyone is upset or confesses to any doubts.

Another counterproductive aspect of many youth groups is the tendency of the adults to dominate discussion. Also, adults are prone to keep moral considerations in the ethereal realm with the result that the application to real-life situations does not register. The sterile church-classroom setting, where a teacher intones a rather pedantic monologue about the doctrines of our religious systems, is almost incapable of instigating the kind of growth we hope to see. These tendencies inhibit the openness and free exchange that Kohlberg believes to be essential for moral growth.

Taking into account the moral development of young people, I would like to propose a general format for tackling significant moral issues in youth ministry. I believe the extra effort will pay dividends by advancing the moral character of young people and enlivening their experience. (Kohlberg concedes that enlightened moral reasoning may not correlate with actual behavior.)

Step 1. *Introduce* the topic. Make them feel it. Provoke them by alluding to the alternatives. Use media creatively, and keep the discussion open-ended.

Step 2. Move into *discussion*. Since the adult leader is merely a facilitator, one who raises questions, probes, and draws out individuals, the leader's own opinions should not be foisted on the group at this point, nor should a premature resolution be allowed.

Step 3. Design an *experience*. Put the topic or problem into a real-life context. Arrange contacts; make specific assignments; and engineer a firsthand experience.

Step 4. *Reflect* on the experience. Challenge each person to formulate his or her own views. Keeping a journal or writing a letter is an excellent medium for this. Drama, role-playing, and other artistic expressions are means of rethinking and interpretation.

Step 5. Tentative *conclusions*. It now becomes appropriate for the adult leaders to share their own biases and opinions. Since the teenagers have already had time to be intellectually and emotionally engaged with the topic, they will be less likely to be intimidated or to mindlessly assent to easy answers.

These steps should be adapted to the maturity level of the group. Although the leaders no longer dominate the process, they have the responsibility to orchestrate a sequence of events that will quite possibly be filled with some surprises. This is exciting, and the prospects of probing beneath superficialities are most promising. Moral maturity is enhanced as we respect the need of adolescents to reach an understanding of, and an independent commitment to, ethical principles. And we must creatively support the venture.

THE ULTIMATE CRISIS

Among young people, the suicide rate has doubled in the last ten years, making it the second leading cause of death after accidents for people between fifteen and twenty-four years of age. Each year about 300,000 teenagers attempt suicide. Fortunately, few succeed. But the several thousand who do succeed constitute a modern American tragedy.[8]

Adolescents have not yet mastered the art of balancing the anxieties and frustrations of life. Their coping mechanisms are not yet firmly in place. The wisdom of experience is not there to offer reassurance and solace, to remind them that "suicide is a permanent solution to a temporary problem."[9] It is surprising that suicide is more the scourge of the well-to-do; pressure to perform and measure up in that social strata can be intense.

Warning signs that indicate a need for help include a direct or indirect threat of suicide, talk of death, frequent drinking, signs of friendlessness, giving away valued possessions, abrupt changes in behavior, or sudden, inexplicable euphoria or whirlwind activity after a spell of gloom. These signs of suicidal depression should not be ignored or dismissed.

Family relationships are, once again, significant. "Parents in the U.S. spend less time with their children than parents of almost any other nation in the world," observes the president of the American Society of Suicidology. The best protection for a suicide-prone child is a close, caring, and considerate family. This will not preclude problems or depression, but it will increase the chances that somebody will notice the malaise and respond to it with concern and support.[10]

Melissa, a lonely and confused fourteen-year-old who had denied she was pregnant for several months, penned this note to her mother just before taking her own life:

> I'm very sorry to put you all through the troubles. I think everything I have to do is done.
> I drank some wine and took some pills. But before I did all that I prayed to my father God in heaven. I asked him to forgive me but he won't. I don't blame him for that.
> Please pray that I won't be sent to hell, because then I won't be able to come back and watch over you and help you. I want to do that.
> Mom, please don't have a nervous breakdown and be crying all the time. I don't want you to. I want you to live

forever and ever, the way you want to and I will always love you very much. Please try and forgive me.

I love you always and always.

Love, Melissa.[11]

QUESTIONS

1. Why are so many adults uncomfortable around adolescents? Can you cite examples of this intergenerational hostility?

2. Are teenagers old children or young adults? What problems does their unique developmental status cause for their parents?

3. How would you respond to Lisa? What does she need?

4. Should youth leaders ever accept the role of substitute parents? What is the relationship between parents and youth leaders?

5. To be behind or ahead in physical development can present a problem. Explain.

6. How do youth leaders decide at what intellectual level to aim their conversations and messages?

7. How does your youth ministry respond to the four identity-status groups? How do you feel about people with these attitudes?

8. How could you apply the findings of Kohlberg to your planning and teaching in the youth-ministry setting? Are you comfortable with moments of "cognitive disequilibrium"?

9. How can we prevent moods of anxiety and depression in young people from leading to suicide? Do you ever have contact with such people?

10. Was adolescence a traumatic experience for you? What were you like then? What kinds of behaviors or dispositions are hard for you to deal with now?

3 CONTEMPORARY CULTURAL TRENDS

Although it is important to discern the developmental phases of adolescence, there is another bit of homework that should be assigned to all youth workers: the task of staying up-to-date with the youth subculture. The interplay of internal struggles and external influences shapes the contours of young people's experience. If we are to be involved, therefore, we need to have a clear picture of this "youthscape."

In one sense, it is futile to attempt to portray accurately the contemporary youth scene; the breadth of the subject is prohibitive, and any analysis would be subject to rapid obsolescence. The youth environment is not static. It is constantly changing. At best, we can only keep pace with it in a general way and hope that our ministry synchronizes with their world as it is today and as it will be tomorrow.

However, I am reluctant to skip it altogether. Some sort of general sketch of contemporary youth culture needs to be made if we are to stay in touch with kids and their agenda. My own observations lead me to suspect that the church is pathetically out of touch with teenagers and, furthermore, blithely ignores or smugly denounces all that the youth may be up to. The church is often years behind in its understanding of the setting and problems of this age group. This ahistorical and otherworldly approach to youth ministry leads to a misreading of their circumstances and the accoutrements of their lifestyle.

My intention is to survey briefly this enchanted subculture, hoping that it might capture some of the flavor of the mid-eighties and spur us to stay with it. To condense a mountain of material, I have chosen to present each topic in summary form.

	The Fifties	**The Sixties**	**The Seventies**
Representative heroes	Ike, Mickey Mantle, Mickey Mouse, Elvis Presley	JFK, M.L. King, Beatles, revolutionaries	Superheroes, Ali, Kiss, Charlie's Angels
Their attributes	safe, bland, conservative	colorful, controversial	fantasy, un-real
Identified with	the "in group": country, school, fraternity	the world: the global vil-lage	the individ-ual
Believed in	technology (materialistic)	mankind (humanistic)	myself (atomistic)
Our villains	communism	the system, the establishment	any outside interference
Drug of prefer-ence	alcohol	LSD	marijuana
Underground counterculture	beatniks	hippies	new age cults
Our goals	comfort, conve-nience, upward mobility	political libera-tion	self-fulfillment
Overall strengths	stable, produc-tive	compassionate, critical thinking	sensitivity, self-awareness
Overall weak-nesses	shallow, com-placent	destructive, ex-hausting	escapist, narcissistic

DIVERGENT DECADES

To know where we are, we need to determine where we have been. Since modernity usually dates itself from the end of

World War II, and since the phenomenon of a separate youth culture is a postwar idea, it will be instructive to examine the three full decades that have elapsed and to study the traits peculiar to each.

The fifties (the mood, not the literal ten-year span) turned into the sixties sometime in 1963 or 1964, heralded by the free-speech movement in Berkeley and the Beatles. The sixties ceased with the end of the Vietnam War and the disillusionment of Watergate in the early seventies.

The introspective seventies retreated from the idealistic activism of the sixties in a dramatic turnabout. The heros of the sixties were either martyred or they dropped out of public view, leaving a barren shelf of pop idols.

In 1977 I asked a class of high-school students to name the heroes of the preceding two decades. Within minutes they had compiled a lengthy list. When I asked for the heroes of the seventies, I was greeted with an embarrassed silence. Finally, they mentioned a couple of cartoon superheroes and celluloid characters, none of whom live out their heroics in the real world. They were fictional heroes who could not be role models in any practical sense.

To plot our present cultural position (a task as frustrating as following a rocket in flight), we need to trace the development of the trends that have emerged out of the late seventies and have spilled over into the eighties. These trends may be clues to determining the complexion of our time.

NEW CONSCIOUSNESS

New Consciousness is a term that describes the proliferating pathways that claim to lead to the realization of one's own potential. This eccentric conglomerate is clearly a product of the seventies. James Sire has distilled three main tenets of this astonishing world view:

 • Each self is the creator of its own universe, and that is the only world that exists for that self.

67

✳• All of reality is manifested in two dimensions: (a) the visible universe accessible through ordinary consciousness, and (b) the invisible universe, which is a separate reality accessible through altered states (such as drugs, meditation, the occult, biopsychic mechanisms).

✳ • The goal is total awareness, not limited by space and time, and transcending all rational judgment.[1]

New Consciousness appeals to young people because (1) it promises to alleviate the boredom of the "straight" world; (2) it overcomes their sense of helplessness as they struggle to gain control of their lives; (3) it resolves the confusion of competing claims; they simply add new beliefs and techniques to their collection; (4) it provides an escape from the threats to their future in this world; and (5) it offers the excitement of exploring forbidden zones.

This amorphous consortium of exotic spirituality is an ingenious blend of Western technology with Eastern mysticism. It is a synthesis that claims to surpass the clinical sterility of science while pumping high voltage into the placid tranquillity of the Orient. For the wandering pilgrims of the seventies this "next stage of human ascent" can be reached by contact (usually a temporary apprenticeship) with any one of a plethora of representative movements (such as parapsychology, est/forum, Yoga, TM, Zen, Eckankar, Lifespring, primaling, rolfing, hypnosis).

The adherents of New Consciousness are of all ages. The writings of Aldous Huxley, the LSD tripping at Harvard in the sixties, and the musings at the Esalen Institute supposedly kicked off the American version of this permeating world view. Its newest converts are generally younger, and more importantly, these beliefs have had a profound influence upon teenagers, though not many could articulate them.

"Tolerance of everything but commitment to nothing." "Try everything at least once, but avoid entanglement with anything." "Don't get locked into a routine . . . stay loose." "Nothing is permanent." "Don't think about it, and it will go away." "Sink the guilt trip." "Who needs the hassle?" "Be true to yourself." "Don't preach." "Let your glands be your guide." These are the slogans smuggled into the youth culture by the advocates of New Consciousness, and they continue to hold sway.

NEOCONSERVATISM

The new conservative trend in our society, is either a moderate corrective to or a vehement backlash against the rampant permissiveness of the late sixties and the seventies—it depends on one's own affiliation. However one defines it, it is diametrically opposed to New Consciousness and all that it stands for.

The concerns of the neoconservatives are down-to-earth and straightforward: (1) They oppose government overregulation; (2) they support the revitalization of the U.S. military and resent its impotence over the past decade; (3) they are concerned about street crime and the leniency shown by the courts; and (4) they have had enough of the weird and the deviant.[2]

They are tired of caring for the "less fortunate" and are hostile toward the paternalistic liberalism of the so-called great society's welfare system. It is time, they proclaim, to regain the rights and opportunities that belong to all real Americans and to end the siege that stymied them in the sixties and seventies.[3]

Neoconservatism hails the return of the straight, the decent, and the ambitious. Bizarre extremes and pushy minorities will no longer be catered to.[4] Furthermore, America will now reassert its dominance on the international scene in the face of communist incursions around the globe. The reelection of Ronald Reagan in 1984 and the eminence of right-wing organizations such as the Moral Majority proved the political clout of the revived conservative coalition, which had wallowed as the silent majority for many years.

The new conservative-reactionary mood among young people cannot be missed. On the surface we have seen hair getting shorter, the growing popularity of country-western music and styles, and the return of draft registration. Less obvious, but of greater consequence, are evidences of open racism, the drive to get ahead and get rich, a swaggering militarism, and the rationalized hypocrisy that often accompanies moralistic crusading. These attitudes are no longer rare among youth.

THE CULTURE OF NARCISSISM

In his important book *The Culture of Narcissism*, Christopher Lasch indicts our culture as being inordinately self-seeking and self-preoccupied. It is a stinging rebuke to the cresting developments of the seventies. His analysis exposes the ironies of what he calls secondary narcissism. Primary narcissism is the egoism characteristic of any normal child; we call it "childish" when an individual regresses to that infantile state. The secondary narcissist (1) appears conceited but actually does not like himself; (2) craves attention but cannot accept love; (3) is dependent on others but resents that dependence; (4) is ravenous for admiration but contemptuous of those he or she impresses; (5) itches for stimulation though there are no objects that can satisfy; (6) is caught up with pseudo-self-insight; (7) is seductive and charming but cool and remote; and (8) is obsessed with image but unconcerned about substance.

The narcissist reduces truth to credibility and reality to perception. The illusion in the mirror is more important than the person reflected. "Nothing succeeds like the image of success." Everyone is a performer (or as Lasch plainly calls it, a prostitute), and life is a theater. In actuality, Lasch explains, it is a war of all against all—our personal lives are battlefields since we are isolated from each other by mistrust. Depth of character has vanished, and the future is drastically foreshortened.[5]

It is possible to view New Consciousness as the left wing and Neoconservatism as the right wing of the Culture of Narcissism. As hostile to each other as they appear to be, both are intent upon a "me first" scenario ("me only" in New Consciousness, "us first" in Neoconservatism). The New Consciousness person is saying, "I am infinite [I am God]." The focus is internal, and some sort of ultimate escape is anticipated. The Neoconservative says, "We must defend ourselves and win back our privileges." The focus is external, and the goal is to fight back and subdue one's enemies.

The flow of these two currents in the mainstream of the eighties can be detected. Whether Neoconservatism will supplant New Consciousness is debatable. There certainly is no consensus except, perhaps, that we are plagued by the character disorders inflicted by narcissism.

THE BIG SQUEEZE

Young people grow up fast these days—probably too fast for their own well-being—but it seems that they are maturing more slowly. They know too much too soon, and the effects of not being able to process all this information is a serious matter.

The "me generation" is cynical, untrusting, and filled with fear. At the same time they still want to believe in something or somebody. The incongruity of this split perspective is illustrated in a segment of a candid interview that took place in the early eighties:

> Interviewer: Will the United States be a better or worse place to live in the next ten years?
>
> Student: The U.S. will definitely be a worse place to live.
>
> Interviewer: Then you must be pessimistic about the future.
>
> Student: No, I'm optimistic.
>
> Interviewer: Why?
>
> Student: Because I have a high grade-point average, and I'm going to get a good job, make a lot of money, and live in a nice house.

Youthful optimism still prevails. But anxieties about the economy, the energy crisis, crime, broken homes, nuclear war, drug abuse, pollution, coupled with self-doubts that have always haunted the adolescent psyche can lead to a fatalistic outlook that fuels and justifies a hedonistic lifestyle. If you are doomed

71

to ride on the Titanic, they might say, at least you can ride first-class.

Dr. Robert Ledge incisively discusses this development:

> The complexities and competitive pressures of modern life combined with the symbols of success being available to practically everyone has produced an anomic condition which manifests itself in self oriented activity.
>
> The specific content of the values which are indicative of this self orientation are traced to the countercultural movement of the Viet Nam war generation. Use of drugs and permissive sexual standards, behaviors which characterize the present generation of youth, represented the means by which the Viet Nam war generation instilled solidarity against the war. Today, drug use and sexual permissiveness symbolize the hedonistic, escapist self orientation which dominates young people of our time.
>
> Faced with the disillusioning events of the past decade coupled with the introspective pressures generated by the anomie of affluence, today's youth have withdrawn from expressing concern about events occurring in society (which they feel helpless to control) to a concern about one's self. It appears that in the modern mass society, escapism and hedonism are symptomatic of the feeling that today people have nothing to believe in—no wars, no causes, no villains, no heroes. All that remains is the overwhelming cynicism of the times due to people's declining faith in the viability of the basic institutions of society.[6]

This void envelopes the children of the eighties. "Keeping busy" and "having fun" are distractions from emptiness. But life for the adolescent can quickly get rough and nasty. The weariness and discontent can be interrupted by a blitzkrieg of crises. Then they must run a tight slalom course at high speed. Mere survival is considered an achievement; being called a "survivor" is the great compliment of the eighties.

To add to the difficulty, things are not always as they seem; some of the obstacles are camouflaged, disguising the danger ahead. The once-reliable maps through this maze are either out-of-date or are consulted without benefit of a pathfinder. Many teenagers are virtually on their own. Adults who have gone before are as likely to mislead as to lead.

The odds of a safe passage are running stiffly against you (even boredom can do you in). That most kids make it is more a tribute to common grace and the resilience of youth than it is to the agencies (such as the family and the church) traditionally counted on to provide guidance and personal support.

A national news magazine's special report released in 1982 summarized the crisis in this way:

> Episodes (of anti-social behavior) point up what many social scientists regard as one of the most significant—and disturbing—trends of recent years: A new generation of American teenagers is deeply troubled, unable to cope with the pressures of growing up in what they perceive as a world that is hostile or indifferent to them.
>
> Among thousands of teenagers, these experts report, alienation and a lack of clear moral standards now prevail to the point where individual lives, families and in some cases whole communities are threatened. To be sure, the vast majority of young Americans emerge from their teenage years—always a troubled period—as well-balanced individuals.
>
> Yet authorities involved with youths from inner cities to suburbia suggest the process rarely if ever has produced such serious disorders—especially among middle-class children seemingly reared with every material advantage. Even those who emerge from adolescence today with few emotional scars undergo stresses far greater than those of earlier generations. As many as a third of the nation's teenagers seem unable to roll with life's punches. They grow up lacking the internal controls needed to stay on course.
>
> Most adolescents seem to share the idea that these are hard times in which to mature to adulthood—harder, they believe, than their parents faced because of a pervasive drug culture and more broken families. Many teens suffer from stress and depression after being bounced from parent to parent after divorce. Youth from middle and upper-income families often wilt under constant urgings to excel in sports or academics, to be popular, to win acceptance to good colleges or to aim for high-paying professional careers. Those in the inner-city remain largely jobless and feel

73

trapped in despair. "Burnouts" languish on street corners, in video-game arcades, in school parking lots. One side effect: A rise in what experts call "sociopathic" subcultures, ranging in membership from far-out cults and extremist groups such as the Ku Klux Klan to the demented punk-rock underground.[7]

Categorizing 23 million teenagers is, admittedly, a risk. Rhetorical and statistical generalizations cannot deal with the specifics of these trends, and they cannot help us predict what is happening in every city and town with every person. These reports, however, can be used as context-setters. They can help us know, in a general way, how to interpret our experiences as we go about the business of ministering to individuals. There is no ministry to charts and graphs, only to live people. At all times we must be with people to check the real meaning of the cross-sectional studies.

CAMPUS CLIQUES

Snug social groupings are always present in adolescent society. If a teenager cannot break into one, he or she castigates it for being a clique. If the teenager does manage to break in, it is considered only an informal group of friends. These groups, or cliques, (depending on your perspective) are strong socializing influences. If the unmet needs of the adolescent are great, the group's power may be near total. For the teenager, these groups are a dress rehearsal for the adult world.

Most cliques have their origins in junior high school. There, kids gather around certain interests. By ninth grade these groups solidify, and by the tenth grade they are highly stabilized (a very difficult time to change schools). By senior year they weaken as a result of diverging interests, plans for the future, and the urge for more freedom. However, these groupings often continue into that glorified high school, the community college.

The nomenclature and configurations of these groups vary, but a typological index can be identified:

Those with *school spirit* (sometimes called *rah-rahs*) are active on athletic teams (the *jocks*), the student council and its committees, and the cheering squads. They are usually affluent, outgoing, all-around kids. They *party,* but their worst offenses are misdemeanors. They are perceived to be at the center of the action and either admired or resented for their status. They are the *socials*.

Those with *academic* inclinations (also known as *brainers,* or *dexters*) are serious about grades and intellectual pursuits. They may be involved in science or language clubs and are disposed to doing concentrated and extracurricular work. They are consciously preparing for higher education and technical careers. They sometimes work hard at shedding their overly serious *nerd* images.

Those with delinquent tendencies are at odds with the institutional purposes and regulations. They cluster in *gangs,* or *tribes,* and make up the *counterculture,* which stands outside of the sanctioned social structure of the school (student government, clubs, teams, homecoming, and proms). A variety of groups make up the counterculture. There are *freaks* (an ambiguous term referring to organic hippy types—an endangered species—or to an incorrigible nonconformist with unconventional interests) and *burnouts* or *dopers* (both hard-core *druggies* or *space cadets*). There are *greasers* (with leather jackets, motorcycles, and the omnipresent cigarette) and *cowboys* (young rednecks wearing boots and dipping chaw) and *punks* (attired in unflattering and incongruous clothing with spiked haircuts). All these groups typify teenage rebellion with its obligatory drug use.[8]

Those whose social lives center around a *special interest* form satellite groups on the campus. A person who belongs to the band or the choir or the drama club or the newspaper, for instance, may find friends and fulfillment in that activity.

Those with a racial or ethnic *minority* identity often find themselves thrown together by choice or by exclusion from the majority group.

Each clique has its own jargon, costumes, customs, and codes. Though there is some overlap, there is not much movement between groups; and the teenagers themselves are quite aware of who fits in where (though there are those who do not fit in anywhere). A demographic map of the campus would reveal a kind of segregation that is enforced with fairly blatant forms of peer pressure.

The kids who do not do well in school and are not successful in the condoned activities are likely to be overlooked or put down by administrators and faculty. A very few gather most of the accolades; a large percentage pass through as matriculation digits, receiving token recognition at best; and a sizeable number are contentious toward the whole system.

In a clever book entitled *Is There Life After High School?* the author divides the student body into the "innies" and the "outies." Most of us are, or were, "outies." But the irony is that high-school society overvalues traits that are of minimal significance in the adult world and undervalues abilities that will be rewarded later on. Physical stature and good looks, athletic ability, ephemeral popularity, wearing the right styles, and driving hot cars will impress others; while intellectual prowess, artistic ability, and depth of character are mostly unappreciated and, perhaps, even an embarrassment if overdone. After graduation, the "innies" face the problem of living up to their high-school performance, while the rest of us struggle to get beyond the failures that we can vividly recall.[9]

THE WRONG STUFF

It would be difficult to contradict the claim that drug abuse is out of control in this country. The decade of the eighties is underway with a looming epidemic of chemical dependency among young people.

There are those who suggest that the real harm is in the enforcement of legislation against "controlled substances." A letter to the editor of *Sports Illustrated,* after that magazine had printed a former player's shattering exposé of the prevalence of cocaine in the National Football League, reflects this glib liberal attitude. The player was a user who had just about blown it all on this drug (the original article, incidentally, was titled "I'm Not Worth a Damn"[10]).

Sir:

It is embarrassing that your publication made such a big play of the Don Reese "special report" on cocaine use in the NFL. . . . Millions of Americans use cocaine as a recreational drug and suffer no lasting ill effects from occasional use. While there are undoubtedly many victims of drug abuse in our society, it is ridiculous to evade personal responsibility the way Reese did and blame the drug. It was (his) own problems that led him to abuse cocaine and ruin a promising athletic career. That he allowed what is for many a harmless diversion to control his life is an indictment of his personality.[11]

Many of us would probably admit to some libertarian impulses. We would agree that incarceration is not fun and that in many cases it is not the best way to deal with the abusers of illicit drugs. But this problem is disrupting the lives of a generation in such a devastating way that to ignore the drug traffic is absolutely irresponsible. Adolescence is difficult enough without the benumbing or agitating (depending on the poison) effects of the current cornucopia of drugs.

The vendors are ubiquitous. Drugs are relatively easy to get, and the price is always right—the first time. (Often the first overture may be made to a kid who is only in the fourth or fifth grade.) Drugs have become so common that they have become acceptable—even to adults. Even the authorities wink at the so-called soft drugs like alcohol and marijuana.

How bad is it? The latest figures do not indicate whether this plague is peaking or receding. But the problem is so widespread that the teenager who does refuse to experiment should be commended for his or her courage to stand alone.

Alcohol. That good old all-American drug is making a smashing comeback. In 1983 Americans drank 179 million barrels of beer, more than 43 six-packs per person![12] Getting drunk, loaded, or wasted (it should be remembered that alcohol is a depressant) is a pastime that has returned with a vengeance. And let there be no mistake—teenagers drink to get drunk. At least 80 percent have tried it; about a third misuse it; and 15 percent are considered problem drinkers and prime candidates

77

to join the ranks of millions of alcoholics in this country.[13] Beer commercials are constantly aired on television and are among the most alluring. As popular as beer drinking is, ignorance about its effects (especially on driving and in combination with other drugs) is widespread.[14] It is interesting that research has deduced that many problem drinkers come from homes where the parents were either moderate-to-heavy drinkers or dogmatic teetotalers (a slap to us dogmatic types). Drinking is known to increase the incidence of fatal auto accidents and violent crime.

Marijuana. This weed is the kindred drug of American youth. Two-thirds of all eighteen-to-twenty-five-year-olds have tried it.[15] It can be demonstrated that this widely tolerated euphoriant can damage lungs, inhibit the body's immunological system, impair memory, and induce a state of lethargy.[16] The motivation-reducing factor may be the most insidious characteristic of grass because teenagers are in a critical time for making decisions and learning skills. As of 1985, studies showed that although the incidence of pot smoking had leveled off, about 6 percent of high-school students used it daily, and 27 percent of the seniors were frequent users. Obviously, continual use of cannabis incurs the greatest risk to health and psychological well-being.

Cocaine. The chic, high-class *lady* was the chemical fad of the early eighties. Coke is the expensive stimulant of celebrities, and this image gives it a prestige among young people. It is the Rolls Royce of illicit drugs. The rush is said to be unbelievable. Perhaps 20 million Americans are snorting, injecting, or freebasing cocaine.[17] In a 1984 study, 16% of high-school seniors said they had tried cocaine at least once. The National Center for Disease Control states that the dangers in cocaine use

> include consequences of both acute and chronic use. Acute toxicity is characterized by nervousness, dizziness, blurred vision and tremors, and may lead to convulsions, cardiac arrythmia and respiratory arrest. Chronic use is associated with ulceration and perforation of the nasal septum ("nose candy" is one of its cute nicknames), weight loss, insomnia, anxiety, paranoia, and hallucination.[18]

One well-heeled addict lamented that cocaine subtly took over his personality.[19]

Amphetamines and *barbiturates*. These uppers and downers are prescription pills. Pep pills, bennies, and speed ("crank") are used to get you high; and all the colors of the rainbow (red and blue devils, yellow jackets), phennies and 'ludes bring you back down. About 10 percent of the high schoolers pop them on those "necessary" occasions.

LSD and *mescaline*. The bad acid trips of the "Strawberry Fields" generation scared off many young explorers of the wilds of "inner space," though hallucinogens are still a part of the drug smorgasbord. Both acid and mesc (peyote) have been touted as mind-expanding drugs. But clinical studies have uncovered a paradox:

> The subject feels he has more insights, is more creative, has more answers to life's problems, but does not or cannot demonstrate them objectively. The overt behavior is not modified, and these new insights are short-lived . . . the products of creative effort under the influence of the drug largely prove to be inferior to those produced before the drug experience. Paintings done in LSD-creativity studies have been reported as reminiscent of schizophrenic art.[20]

PCP. This animal tranquilizer literally drives people crazy, and fortunately, the angel dust madness of the late seventies has subsided. Periodically some bright entrepreneur markets a hip new drug that those walking along the edge have to try—and the fatalities are recorded before research can even verify the harm done.

Heroin. With the bad press given this archdevil of all drugs, we might be misled into believing that only a few wretched addicts still exist. In fact, probably more than 500,000 Americans are hooked on this deadly narcotic (the heroin addict has an average life expectancy of five years), or about one of every four hundred people. In New York City one in every forty residents is jamming a needle into his or her veins.[21] It is the ultimate kick and an inevitable temptation to the already-old young person with a season pass for the not-so-merry-go-round.

Look-alikes or designer drugs. The spirit of enterprise cannot resist cashing in on the multibillion dollar drug business, especially if the legal risks can be avoided. Look-alikes are fake amphetamines (often labeled *speed*) that are disguised to resemble the real thing. The real danger is in taking a megadose of a substance like caffeine unwittingly, which can have lethal consequences.[22]

Cigarettes. Approximately 20 percent of teenagers are smokers. The number of boys that smoke has declined during the past ten years, while the girls have been catching up ("You've come a long way, baby"). Studies have found that boys smoke to cope with social situations, while it is a sign of independence for girls. The main predictor for individuals is whether or not their same-sex friends smoke.[23]

The Surgeon General has stated that substance addiction is the nation's number-one preventable health hazard. It usually starts during the teenage years. No one ever intends to be ensnared, but statistics warn that opening the door to experimentation is replete with serious risks. Adolescence is challenging enough without drugs.

Youth leaders must look beyond national trends and try to assess their own regions and communities, although they should also be aware that no place is immune to this problem now endemic in the youth culture. Drugs—powerful drugs—are out in the back alleys of the ghetto and on suburban streets and even country roads. It has burgeoned into a big business worth more than 100 billion dollars a year in the United States.[24] Drugs have had a detrimental effect on the schools, athletics, the armed forces, the entertainment field, and the family. And the youth minister who does not see this is living in a fool's paradise.

TEENAGE SEX

Nearly half of all fifteen-to-nineteen-year-olds have participated in premarital sex. The average age of the first sexual experience is sixteen. One million teenage girls—about one in ten—get pregnant each year, mostly outside of marriage. Some

1.3 million children are being raised by teenage mothers—about half of whom are unmarried.[25] Some of these young mothers believe that having a child is the best way to get the loving attention of their parents or boyfriend.

The much vaunted sexual revolution of the past decade is bearing fruit in this generation. Not everyone is involved (many teenagers never date at all during high school), but there is a new casual attitude toward sex. Even "recreational sex" is not considered an aberrant practice. The culture shames those who wish to remain virgins. Whether the conservative reaction against an overly permissive society will halt or reverse this trend remains to be seen. Will there be a "new celibacy"?

The popular media assume that any romantic relationship should be physically consummated if the couple is reasonably normal. Married sex is boring (for example, a recent analysis revealed that only 6 percent of the acts of intercourse implied on television soap operas involved married couples).[26] When Mother Teresa addressed Harvard University's commencement in 1982, she advised the graduates to preserve their virginity until marriage. The audience—with all due respect to her legendary charity in India—was incredulous. It is not even an issue anymore.

The adolescent of the eighties must contend with an apparent conspiracy against the responsible management of sexuality. Parents (even relatively mature and sophisticated parents) are embarrassed or too late with their lectures. Sex education in the schools has attempted to present the facts in a "value-free" manner. The streets are buzzing with the latest misinformation (two-thirds of the teenage girls who are sexually active never or only erratically use birth-control devices). The movies, television shows, commercials, and the lyrics of popular songs emphasize, often explicitly, the physical dimension of relationships.

Added to this outside pressure is the sexual drive itself—as yet undefined and unchanneled—and the teenager must learn to cope with all of this. There is a new kind of honesty about sex, an honesty that has replaced such hypocrisies of yesteryear as the double standard, the shotgun wedding, and private lust. But this honesty has also caused a kind of depersonalization of sexual activity that cannot altogether repress that wistful question, "Will you still love me tomorrow?"

The dilemmas posed by adolescent sexuality are amplified in this reflection by a seventeen-year-old girl.

> The most difficult situation with which I had to cope was when my boyfriend asked me to have sex with him. I love him and didn't want to hurt him by saying no, making him feel rejected, but I didn't want to hurt myself by saying yes.
>
> Every time he approached me with that question, I told him I didn't want to and usually clammed up. So, one day I sat down to write him a long letter explaining how I felt. In my letter, I told him I didn't feel I had to have sex with him and if he felt I did then something was wrong. I also said I didn't want to be just another girl he could make it with. I want to be me, myself, and not some object.
>
> The next day I dropped off my letter at his work, half-hoping he would be there, half-hoping he wouldn't. I was nervous and upset. I didn't want him to think this was the end of our relationship.
>
> After work we were to see a movie, but instead we went to have coffee. Coffee we had, but talk we didn't. We both didn't know what to say. I knew he was upset, just looking at him I could tell. So we went to his house, listened to records, and attempted to talk. I told him that I have my values and he has his. I said that I may change my mind in a couple of years or months. He said he understood.
>
> A couple of days later my mother stopped me in the hall and told me it was time I had a talk with her. I slowly followed her to her room. She then proceeded to talk to me about contraceptives, and told me no matter what she says, it won't stop me from having sex with my boyfriend. I laughed and told her she had nothing to worry about. I told her how I talked with my boyfriend and things are OK.
>
> Well, months have gone by, in fact, five, to be exact. I have changed my mind. My boyfriend and I went to a local gynecologist and asked for an appointment for a physical and a talk on birth-control methods. After much consideration I chose to take the pill. I was apprehensive, with all the

ill side effects, but the doctor convinced me it was safe because I was young, healthy, didn't smoke.

My parents don't know, but his do. His parents are glad that we are both sensible in taking the right means to protect ourselves. They understand how we feel. My parents may have an idea of what's going on but I think they are afraid to approach me with it.

I'm not worried, though. I love my boyfriend and he loves me. But I can't help but doubt his love for me. I'm insecure and need his love. I let him know and he's thankful for that. He is honest and forthright . . . I have coped with this most difficult situation but it's been hard.[27]

Teenagers in love, with the attendant sexual temptation, should be viewed with sympathy.

Tragically, many adolescents are victimized by adult predators. Pornography is a big business in this country. Kiddie porn (luring subjects six to sixteen years old into its seamy underworld) is estimated to be 10 to 20 percent of the pornography market. Belatedly, the Supreme Court has issued a ruling that will help curtail this repugnant form of exploitation.

Nothing is more difficult to discuss than incest, although even this taboo is now being more widely talked about. One in ten, maybe more, females are sexually abused by an adult before puberty, and in many cases, the abuse continues for years.[28] Incest is never the fault of the children (they are too trusting, too frozen by fear), but its consequences of depression, anger, and the dampening of normal heterosexual drives are theirs to bear.

Runaways are particularly vulnerable to sexual exploitation. The one million children under the age of eighteen who run away from home every year (or who are driven from home) are likely to be duped by hustlers, pushers, pimps, and *chickenhawks* (pedophiles who befriend young people fresh off the bus or train and alone in the big city) who are on the lookout for slave labor or worse.

ROCK MUSIC

Rock-and-roll (as it used to be called) provides the anthems of the younger generation. It is their music, and the adult who rebukes its excesses had better be prepared for a retaliatory assault; "Rock-and-roll is here to stay!" has been the standard retort for thirty years. It is an indigenous, inspiring sound and one of the most obvious signatures of the youth culture. Exactly what rock music is has become an intriguing question. But popular music—regardless of its innovations and meanderings—remains the igniting auditory cue for teenagers.

Pages 86 and 87 contain an abbreviated history of rock.

Rock music is tailor-made for the adolescent. It is energetic, emotionally effusive, demonstrative, and edgy in its rebellious attitudes toward adult wisdom and dominion. Hard-driving guitar riffs, a pounding beat, soaring falsettos, and hoarse growls simulate the ecstatic highs and despairing lows of adolescent experience. Teen romance, rebellion, and the latest fads are the major themes. Sometimes the lyrics are mindlessly trite; at times they are poignant and moving; and many times there is no intended message at all. But rock is always evocative. It is the quintessential mood music.

The violence explicit in the Punk–New Wave revision of the original fifties explosion is, by any account, a foreboding chapter in the continuing saga of rock music. Punk is a death trip. Many thought the tamer adaptations of New Wave, its more commercial offspring, would put frenetic Punk out of its misery. But the zombies still walk among us: Black Flag, Johnny Rotten, The Plasmatics, The Dead Kennedys (gruesome is in), and other gar(b)age bands skip quality and go for the all-out shock treatment.[29] Outrageous attire, staged violence, allusions to Satan (explicit or via backward masking), and gratuitous vulgarity are all part of the bizarre show. The nihilism is nearly absolute. For many teenage patrons—the terminally turned off—these antics are no game. Second-generation Punk now resorts to contrivances, bleeding this anti-art form while the posed agony and feigned insanity are still newsworthy.

The music scene is definitely fragmented. Hyphenated rock

(such forms as reggae-rock, synth-rock, art-rock) predominates. Nobody knows for sure where it is going, but seething competition for the spotlight continues. Some critics consider much of today's studio recordings to be a rehash of earlier successes; an entire phalanx of superstars is still riding the momentum of their pasts. Is rock music, as we have known it (and loved or hated it), lurching into its senescence?

VIDEO MANIA

By the time a young person graduates from high school, he or she will have watched about 18,000 hours of television (the typical set is on 7 hours every day). This compares with 12,000 hours spent in the classroom and perhaps 2000 hours in a church setting. Criticism of this medium has been raining down recently, and it can be condensed to the following list of complaints:

- TV is a passive medium. It is not interactive; it does all the work for you. There is no imaginative or creative challenge.
- TV isolates people from each other, even when they are sitting in the same room watching together.
- TV replaces constructive work and play.
- TV does not reflect the real world.
- TV watching makes it difficult to adjust to another environment that does not entertain but demands participation, such as the classroom.
- People can develop a psychological dependence upon having the set on.
- TV probably encourages some people to commit antisocial acts (such as violence).
- Cable TV sneaks soft-core pornography past the censors into our living rooms.

Psychologist and commentator Tom Cottle adds this thought on the topic:

> The more television children watch, the lower their achievement in school. It doesn't matter what they watch—it's just the sheer number of hours. . . . Another study

85

The Roots of Rock

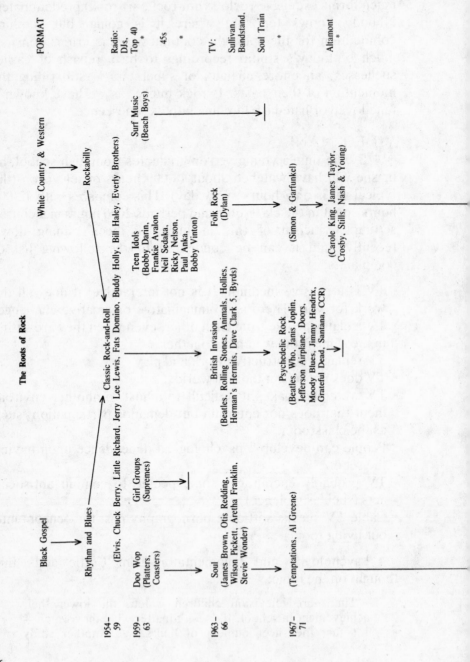

FORMAT

Radio:
DJs,
Top 40 *

45s *

TV:
Sullivan,
Bandstand.
Soul Train *

Altamont *

White Country & Western

Rockabilly

Surf Music
(Beach Boys)

Classic Rock-and-Roll
(Elvis, Chuck Berry, Little Richard, Jerry Lee Lewis, Fats Domino, Buddy Holly, Bill Haley, Everly Brothers)

Teen Idols
(Bobby Darin,
Frankie Avalon,
Neil Sedaka,
Ricky Nelson,
Paul Anka,
Bobby Vinton)

Folk Rock
(Dylan)

(Simon & Garfunkel)

(Carole King, James Taylor,
Crosby, Stills, Nash & Young)

Black Gospel

Rhythm and Blues

Girl Groups
(Supremes)

Doo Wop
(Platters,
Coasters)

British Invasion
(Beatles, Rolling Stones, Animals, Hollies,
Herman's Hermits, Dave Clark 5, Byrds)

Psychedelic Rock
(Beatles, Who, Janis Joplin,
Jefferson Airplane, Doors,
Moody Blues, Jimmy Hendrix,
Grateful Dead, Santana, CCR)

Soul
(James Brown, Otis Redding,
Wilson Pickett, Aretha Franklin,
Stevie Wonder)

(Temptations, Al Greene)

1954–
59

1959–
63

1963–
66

1967–
71

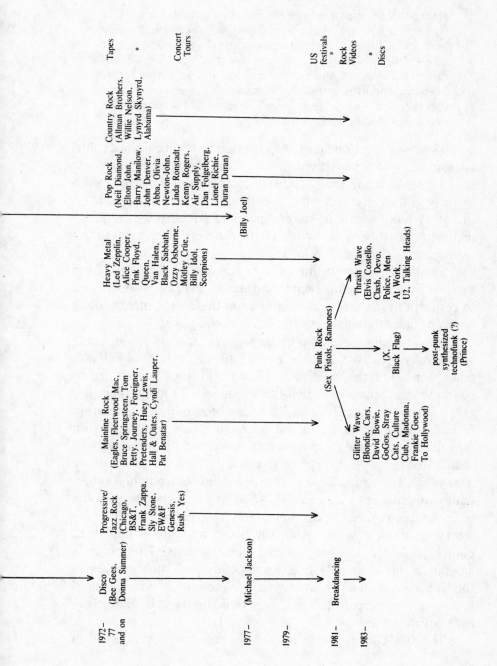

showed that the more television you watch, the more frightened you are about living. But what I guess I really believe is, there is a cheapening quality—a cheapening of this culture—which is very sad for me. . . . All we are interested in is sex and aggression. . . . It's appealing to the hormones and the muscles . . . mindless, superficial, tasteless. We are a very angry people and we are a people who confuse sexuality with intimacy.[30]

The National Educators Association is severe in its denunciation of television programming and commercials. Their spokespeople argue that adolescence is a period when people learn who they are and what they feel, and that television, on the other hand, deals in stereotypes and trivializes experience instead of portraying real characters who verify the truth of the teenagers' subjective emotions.

Furthermore, television advertisements teach kids to cover up their insecure feelings with a cosmetic layer of products and to conform to the group no matter what the cost. Gaining social approval and immediate gratification are the goals.[31]

Movie going remains popular with teenagers. Adolescents between twelve and twenty make up nearly half of all film admissions. For the most part, Hollywood films have failed to characterize teenagers in real-life situations,[32] though there are some noteworthy exceptions. A deluge of mindless exploitation films has been released in the past few years, cashing in on audiences' apparent taste for crass humor and juvenile voyeurism. Movies such as *Porky's, Class of '84, Angel, Private School,* and *Screwballs* are so artless and indisputably antifemale—degrading of all humans—that anyone who cares in the least for teenagers (or for humanity, in general) cannot help worrying about a society that shells out millions of dollars to chortle and leer at these wretched productions. This binge is similar to the seemingly endless popularity of such movies as the *Halloween* and *Friday The 13th* series in which stupid brutalities are perpetrated against screaming teens by indestructible psychopaths.

The studios, of course, have been fabulously successful in

producing high adventure, which appeals to young theater attenders. The *Star Wars* saga, *Jaws,* the *Rocky* and *Superman* series, *E.T., Raiders of the Lost Ark,* and *The Temple of Doom* have been big box-office hits. The special effects are breathtaking.

Video games are commanding many hours of attention from youth as the machines (including home sets) become more available. Computerized space-age games project an alternate, miniaturized world. Many adults may find themselves excluded from these leisure activities, which were brought to us courtesy of high-tech software.

All of these trends suggest that the adolescents of the eighties are more accustomed to responding to images than words. The decline of English language proficiency scores over the past fifteen years foreshadowed this development. Functional illiteracy is a fact.[33] Programs to reinstitute the fundamentals of learning run the risk of being viewed as anachronistic in the computer age. Reading and writing and manual computing are no longer critical skills, and the old-fashioned practice of taking pencil to paper may soon be outmoded and replaced by advanced-capacity cerebral surrogates. The youth leader who does not grasp the extent of this communications revolution will have difficulty understanding adolescents.

CULTS

The New Age cults (Moonies, Hare Krishna, Rajneesh, and other hybrid Eastern imports) are flourishing. Unlike the established home-grown cults such as the Mormons, Jehovah's Witnesses, and Christian Scientists, these groups target young people as prospective members, usually older adolescents aged seventeen to twenty-four.

The most likely recruits are from nominally religious homes where few definite convictions are taught. The adolescents are warmly invited to a free dinner or workshop where they are impressed with an idealistic message that "clears up" a muddled view of the chaotic world. The overtures of friendship are so sincere that they cannot be refused. *Noninformed consent* is the term used to describe this kind of conversion.

Once enfolded into the cult, the individual's identity is given over to the invincible group and its all-knowing leader. Strict rules provide a security not available in the outside world, and the individual is urged to renounce all ties outside the group.

The function of the proselyte is basically twofold: to recruit new members and to make money for the organization. Members accept the right of the cult to think for them and are kept busy most of the day.[34] This is a small price to pay for salvation and a glimpse of the dawning of the new age.

BACK TALK

In evaluating these currents in society and within the less stable adolescent subculture, two considerations must be honored: (1) Due to the progress in communications over the past thirty years, America has developed a pervasive mass culture. Kids in New England and Southern California and the Midwest are simultaneously exposed to the same information via the popular media. Mitigating demographic differences only slightly modify this homogenizing force. (2) But there is also an undeniable, irreducible, and mystifying human factor that precludes any precision in our surveys or predictions; that is, people are not determined by their environment (nor are they preprogrammed by their hormones). Teenagers are not lemmings, though, at times, they may act like sheep. They are wondrously complex and always on the move. Multidimensional individuals, subcultures within subcultures, and a frantically dynamic microcosm make youth ministry an adventure without parallel.

To conclude this chapter, I would like to risk some sweeping generalizations about the decade of the eighties:

The Eighties

Representative heroes	computers, E.T., Harrison Ford, Matt Dillon, J.R. Ewing, John Paul II, Ronald Reagan
Their attributes	cool, nervy, adventuresome
Identify with	"my own kind"
Believe in	my own abilities, opportunities, allied with high-tech
Our villains	nukes, unseen forces
Drug of preference	cocaine
Underground counterculture	punks
Our goals	survival, security
Overall strengths	guts, nerve
Overall weaknesses	loss of meaning, programmed thinking

QUESTIONS

1. Are you a "child" of one of these decades? Can you identify in yourself some of the qualities of the era you grew up in?

2. Give illustrations of contacts you have had with New Consciousness. Can you detect its influence in your community?

3. Is the Neoconservatism of the eighties a corrective to the deviance of the seventies, or does it create new problems? Can you see the influence of this cultural trend in your youth group?

4. What is the difference between narcissism and a healthy self-esteem?

5. How can kids be cynical about the future of the world and be optimistic about their individual prospects? Is that good?

6. Is youth ministry concerned with helping young people survive the eighties? Is survival by itself success?

7. Have you observed the demographic niches and tribal territories of the youth culture? Can you relate across cultural boundaries? Should youth ministries try to break up cliques?

8. Why are junior-high and high-school campuses artificial environments? How have your status and values changed since graduation?

9. How would you confront a young person who is casually experimenting with "recreational" drugs? Would it make any difference if this individual claimed to be a Christian?

10. Is it difficult for a teenager, these days, to manage sexuality? With what pressures and temptations are they contending?

11. Does contemporary rock music have any redeeming value? What concerns do you feel compelled to warn kids about? Why? Is rock-'n'-roll here to stay?

12. Have you adapted your approach to youth ministry to the video-image generation? Should you?

13. How could you modify the author's conjectures about the eighties to fit your setting? What does your analysis suggest in terms of new direction for ministry?

4 SOUNDINGS

As Christian youth workers become more aware of adolescent development and current social trends, they will also better understand the need to fashion a ministry that can deal with the broadest possible spectrum of concerns. Our response to the values and problems of the contemporary youth subculture will reveal our deepest personal convictions. It may be instructive, therefore, to consider several options for interpreting this body of information and to attempt to apply our outlook to some specific cases.

CHRIST AND CULTURE

Richard Niebuhr provides the classic paradigm for assessing a Christian's attitude toward culture.[1] There are four ways to view the relationship between Christ and culture:

1. *Christ against culture.* This view believes that the culture is so hopelessly corrupt that our only choice is an absolute either-or, all-or-nothing decision. We must separate ourselves from this evil world. The early church often found itself in this position during the first two centuries due to the persecution inflicted by hostile religious and political systems.

A youth ministry with this attitude would constantly try to create alternative situations and activities for its young people, warning them away from the popular features of their peer culture. The youth program would schedule events to compete with worldly amusements (a youth social on Friday night, for instance, to prevent attendance at the school basketball game and dance). The dress code, vocabulary, and customs would be in conscious opposition to those of their secular counterparts.

Although I do not subscribe to this separatist style of ministry, I do recognize its devout and even, occasionally, prophetic concern for faithfulness and purity. I do not believe that we can guarantee such virtues by isolating ourselves and young people from the world, but I understand the impulse to do so. The possibility of corruption is real. Although overprotection does not instill maturity, it is preferable to losing someone.

However, fighting the culture is generally not the best way. Forcing teenagers to choose between their friends and Jesus usually imposes an unfair and unnecessary dilemma (disassociation may be necessary in extreme circumstances). It tends to overlook legitimate activities and misses opportunities to minister to the young people who still need to be reached.

2. *Christ of culture*. This view perceives a substantial agreement, or overlap, between the Kingdom of God and modern American culture. If the first view is too pessimistic, this perspective is unbounded in its optimism regarding the glorious usefulness of cultural forms.

A youth ministry reflecting this cheery outlook will bless the latest trends and add its own socializing function to the general mix. Having a good time and helping kids adjust are the vague aims of this civil-religious program. Confrontation with the culture is rare, and normally an endorsement of the status quo is implied. Ministry becomes virtually anything we do.

This approach, it seems to me, underestimates the prevalence of sin and conflict, and it dilutes ministry to the level of mild do-good chaplaincy. Teenagers need direction, but under these conditions no one thinks to offer it.

3. *Christ above culture*. This belief views the affairs of men to be neatly divided into sacred and secular compartments, and never the twain shall meet. Our life in the Spirit is lived by different rules than our daily life in the real world. This dualism assigns us roles to play according to the institutional setting.

The youth minister with this understanding will see to it

that teenagers receive the proper religious instruction without bothering too much with outside concerns. Insuring that the youth passes through the fixed stations of faith is the church's interest. What happens the other six days is mostly irrelevant and beyond the sphere of the rather aloof youth leader in any case.

This viewpoint simplifies the duties of ministry; at the same time, it disregards any wholistic approach to the gospel. It sanctifies hypocrisy and leaves us with an anemic perversion of Christianity. Furthermore, kids are likely to lose interest in the ceremonial aspects unless they have a strong traditional attachment.

4. *Christ transforming culture.* This approach is modeled on the Incarnation. It does not deny that culture needs to be changed, but it does not flinch from engagement.

Youth ministry, according to this theory, will be interested in every facet of the kids' lives. The minister will enter their world with every intention of being an instrument of God's transforming love. He or she is more than willing to work within the cultural system but reserves the right to challenge practices contrary to the well-being of adolescents.

We must recognize the following implications of this approach if we desire to operate effectively from this fourth premise: (a) Each of us is part of our culture—we have our roots in it; we are influenced by it to some degree; and we are called to remain in it; (b) we need to become conversant with the youth culture as it is; (c) we need to evaluate critically the elements of this culture; (d) we must become comfortable in it—participating, relating, and even enjoying our involvement; and (e) we must, paradoxically, remain ever restless; we are sojourners in this world and acknowledge that Christ transcends every cultural form.

In sum, we are compelled to exhibit both pessimism and optimism. We are realistic about human nature and its predilection for waywardness. Yet we cannot be robbed of a hope that dares to believe that redemption is always a possibility (it is not up to us to make final judgments). Because of Christ's work in the world and in us, we are enabled to make a difference in the lives of young people we meet.

ROCK OF AGES

Rock music is, perhaps, the primary purveyor of youth culture. Its jargon, vitality, and mystique screen out the uninitiated so that the code is preserved. Christians in this country are still not sure what to do with popular music; the intramural debate rages on. Often, our pious pronouncements indicate a clash of cultural preferences instead of any moral or metaphysical distinctions. Is there really such a thing as a Christian chord or a pagan rhythm?

Of course, the contemporary rock scene is a mixed bag. Raunchy lyrics and distorted dissonance do not deserve our approval. The sordid lifestyle of some rock celebrities is distasteful. On the other hand, the instrumental artistry, poetic craftsmanship, and universal truths expressed by many performers should be hailed.

The solution, I believe, is not to condemn the entire genre. That would be indiscriminate and tactically unwise. But to automatically accede to an industry that produces whatever will sell is hardly responsible either. We should not say yes or no in advance but should retain the right to judge the individual product on the merits of its own artistic integrity.

That Christ can make use of this controversial medium is confirmed by the multitude of professional musicians who work comfortably within this form and also convey an authentic message of faith, hope, and love.[2] Christian adaptation of a popular idiom is not without its hazards (unabashed egotism being one of them), but if we carefully monitor the frequency and do not countenance moral compromise, we have an obligation to exploit this primal wavelength.

Now, what about the seamy side of rock? If invited by a group of teenagers, should we accompany them to a hard-rock concert of questionable value, to endure, for example, the likes of Cheap Trick, Twisted Sister, Iron Maiden, the purple Prince, or Mötley Crüe? That is a loaded question, but the kind that youth leaders have to face (unless we cloister ourselves away so that the opportunity never arises).

It seems to me that our first responsibility is to estimate the prospects for ministry in this setting. What is least relevant is our own musical taste—that ought to be set aside for the higher purposes of ministry and never be mistaken for an absolute standard or imposed on others.

I would be flattered if the kids saw me as "normal" enough to be interested in going with them and not be a drag on their plans. If the situation seems new and strange—and, therefore, unsettling to us—we need to stretch our capacity for involvement. If the youth minister fears being "stumbled" by attending, he or she should probably avoid the concert but recognize this as immaturity and strive to get past it.

If we go (I would probably go with them, although I would not bring a group as a sponsored event), we need to make the most of the evening. Conversation throughout the evening, especially afterward about the meaning of the performance, could be constructive as long as the youth minister does not come off as a sanctimonious censor.

My hesitation to accept includes such concerns as the expectations of parents, whether I feel I should contribute money to enrich the coffers of sleazy pop stars, and the extent to which an orgy of decibels or drugs might curtail my access to the people I am with. During the evening I would want to spend time interacting with my friends. However, if I felt I had to turn them down, I would certainly affirm my appreciation for their invitation. When I consider the question of going to a rock concert, other questions echo in my mind: "Would I have dined with that despicable tax collector, Zacchaeus? What about my reputation? Should we not avoid all appearances of evil?"

RECREATIONAL SEX

The church habitually moralizes about sexual behavior. The only thing worse than these petty pronouncements is the supposedly enlightened response: "It's not that important; do whatever pleases you, as long as it doesn't hurt anyone." In the process we have almost forgotten the exalted view of human sexuality proposed in Scripture. It is precisely this profound respect, devoid of snippy moralism, that motivates our concern for the adolescent's developing sexuality.

Is premarital sex premature? The conclusions of Erik Erikson would seem to suggest that it is. Sex is usually more of a game among adolescents. They are not yet prepared for true intimacy, and they are experimenting with a tentative identity. Since their values have not yet crystallized, they cannot very well exercise them in an area that demands a thoughtful application of them.

Adolescents are capable of the experience, but not of the adult bonding. Sex is most often a private experience for the teenager—one that, many times, is less pleasurable than the fantasy. Someone has described teenage sex as "mutual masturbation." The emphasis on sensation over deep emotional sharing is not conducive to personal growth, from almost any perspective.

Our pro-sex/pro-responsibility stand does not exempt us from struggling with the bewildering questions raised by teenagers in the throes of the tempest. Defining who I am and what I want in relationships with the opposite sex is a maddeningly difficult project fraught with overwhelming pressures and inevitable failures. At the same time we describe and model the way of fulfillment authored by the creator, we also must express acceptance as Jesus did to those who had fallen. In actuality, we all have fallen, and that realization will deliver us from sitting in self-righteous judgment.

PROBLEM BEHAVIOR

When a teenager has a problem that is bringing harm to himself or herself and others, whether that problem is developmental in nature or environmentally related, the youth leader should respond appropriately. That response is shaped in a moral context and makes a practical appraisal of the long-term physical, emotional, social, and spiritual consequences of the behavior. The response is balanced by a demonstration of compassion that is more interested in helping than in being proven right. The following guidelines are for youth workers who are striving to relieve the hurt and restore the teenager in crisis:

- Gain an understanding of the facts by corroborating the allegations and rumors.
- Be unshockable, without being callous.
- Determine the source of the difficulty: is it the family, peer influence, a cultural factor, a system of authority, a particular individual, the result of another personal problem? Is the trouble continuing as a deliberate, conscious decision? (Be sure that a problem exists and that it is not simply a matter of an adult taking offense.)
- Look beyond the difficulties the person is causing for others, and see the need.
- Do not condemn; do not gossip among other adults in a pejorative manner.
- Do not avoid the person. Time does not heal all wounds; it tends to aggravate or harden them.
- Do not lapse into pity. It is dehumanizing and falsely absolves us from doing anything.
- Listen attentively to her or his side of the story.
- Do not accept his or her conclusions at face value (such smoke screens as "Don't worry, I'm all right!").
- Be patient—a sense of timing is important; listen to the signals. Be certain that our need to rescue is not in charge.
- Do not wait too long; do not be afraid to act.
- Do not expect to be welcomed.
- Do not expect gratitude.
- Expect some resistance, perhaps even anger.
- Remember that there is a lot of self-hatred buried beneath the attacks on the interloping adult.
- Be available to the person—earn a reputation as a good listener, as someone who cares. Be a regular on her or his turf so that there is an excuse for an encounter.

- Be up-front about the facts and our feelings about what is happening; solicit a response.
- Be committed to finding a solution and to being a part of the remediation process, as long as it takes.
- Seek to help the parents and other family members if they are affected by the problem.
- Be prepared to marshal the available resources, to advocate on behalf of a wounded adolescent, and even to battle if unjust obstacles will not budge.
- Though other agencies and professionals may be engaged, never withdraw from personal contact.
- Endeavor to mainstream the person, when he or she is ready, especially into the youth group.

I call this the ministry of creative interference. Only fools—and youth counselors—rush in. But this kind of salutary intervention is the mark of an effective youth ministry that goes beyond a benign neglect of troubles unrelated to the youth program. In this way we touch adolescents where they live. If this sounds like a lot of effort, it is. But it breaks down barriers and penetrates the surface so that the healing power of the gospel is released.

This kind of involvement goes further than traditional counseling. Each problem is addressed in a real-life setting, in the context of a natural and continuing relationship, and with a battery of human and suprahuman resources brought to bear. The youth minister becomes a friend and, as a counselor, "comes along side of" (which is what the verb "to comfort" signifies in Greek) the young person in need. To allow other institutional, program, or narrowly specialized discipling roles to eclipse this trust is to diminish the power of ministry.

THE CULTURE OF NARCISSISM
AND THE WAY OF SELF-DENIAL

Christian discipleship is the antidote to the narcissistic tendencies in all of us. The shallowness, selfishness, cynicism, and decadence of our culture have also invaded our lives and that awareness, for those of us in youth ministry, is particularly depressing. We, too, have been polluted and must redouble our determination to purge these harmful dispositions from ourselves and to instigate a Christian counterculture among our young people (the tension between cultural accommodation and direct combat is always with us). Sensitivity to this struggle for authenticity in the midst of duplicity, fraud, and despair should be cultivated by anyone in ministry.

The well-reasoned prophetic critique of dubious attitudes that have been assimilated by the religious sector begs for a full hearing. The quotes below illustrate such self-critical thinking. In a sense, it is appropriate for Christians to temporarily enforce a double standard; we expect the world to live like the world and are not daunted when that logic is acted out, but we demand of ourselves—we who profess allegiance to Jesus Christ—that we be overtly on the way toward conforming to His image. We should harken to these timely reprimands:

> How is it possible that upwards of 50 million Americans profess to have experienced the regenerative power of new life in Christ and yet are not permeating the world with the values of Christ? Some reasons for failure quickly spring to mind: Much contemporary teaching and literature pays no more than lip service to the real meaning of servanthood and commitment. "Love one another as I have loved you," Christ commands. For him, that meant laying down his life; it can mean no less for us. Simplistic "Jesus saves" and "Heaven is yours now!" messages saturate the media and adorn automobile bumpers. It is superficial and perhaps this accounts for the little impact we have. Our fascination with such miracles as healing deformed limbs obscures for us the greatest miracle of all—that the Word became flesh. Such a Gospel depends, it seems today, not on revealed truth, but on showmanship. (Charles Colson, Prison Fellowship)[3]

> Aren't we scared to death that the Master of the house will return in the midst of our great big American Christian party of self-indulgence and demand an accounting of our stewardship? (Joe Bayly, author, columnist)[4]

> In this country's so-called morality movement, commendable as it is, I find a disturbing degree of ambivalence and

not a few contradictions. For one thing, I observe that it selects moral issues on a highly individualistic and subjective basis. Issues picked for a demonstration of moral concern do not cover the full biblical spectrum. Rather they seem to reflect a preoccupation with middle-class values. . . . In other words, evangelicals can be remarkably sanguine about issues which seriously affect the rest of the world but do not directly touch us. (Stan Mooneyham, Christian humanitarian, statesman)[5]

External freedom is not a self-sufficient end of people and societies. No less than outer freedom, man needs unpolluted space for his spirit, room for mental and moral concentration. Regrettably, contemporary civilized freedom is reluctant to leave us this kind of space. Regrettable, in recent decades our very idea of freedom has diminished and grown shallow in comparison with previous ages; it has been relegated almost exclusively to freedom from outside pressure, to freedom from state coercion. . . . Freedom consists in self-restraint and in full consciousness of responsibility. (Alexander Solzhenitsyn, author, exiled Russian dissident)[6]

Such astute and piercing comments heighten the suspense of living and working in sharp cognizance of two incompatible kingdoms. A concerted effort to create and build an indigenous ministry that is consistent with the indisputable dictates of God's holiness is our avowed goal.

STRIPPED DOWN FOR ACTION

In the light of our analysis of widespread deficiencies of character, there are qualities that ought to distinguish the person wanting to work with youth today. The youth minister should be:

Morally disciplined. For example, it is my impression from reading the Bible that adults are permitted to drink alcohol in moderation. But alcohol abuse is a horrendous problem among young people. If my drinking provides even a lame excuse for a teenager to imbibe, I would rather forgo my freedom. To be straight (which does not mean dull and joyless) is to be a remarkable exception these days.

Responsible in following through on commitments. Among

adolescents "yes" means "maybe" and "maybe" means "probably not." Even among adults, we prefer to keep our options open and not be tied down to anything. A reliable person is a rare find.

Nonmaterialistic. Everyone else is grabbing, and no one has the courage to buck the propaganda and give. Generosity is attractive, especially in the uptight zone where it is every man for himself.

Nonaddicted. Everybody is hooked on something, it seems. Life has gotten so tough that we all need some chemical to get us by. Freedom from such compulsion removes handicaps from living and service.

Honest. Many of us work the truth to our own advantage. Directness, devoid of manipulating schemes, is always refreshing.

Reality-based. Reality is either too unstimulating or too threatening. Escape is possible in an array of nowhere-bound vehicles. Someone who revels in reality, who seems to cope in the middle of all the problems, is a sign of hope.

People-oriented. We are self-absorbed and obsessed with things. A relational style that takes people seriously has a chance of breaking into the isolated, emotion-proof cubicles to which we all have withdrawn.

Spirited. To be cool and guarded with occasional irrational outbursts is typical. To protect ourselves we do not entrust our feelings to anyone. After a while our ability to feel strongly starts to atrophy. Spontaneity, sincere enthusiasm, and emotional engagement bring warmth and color into a world jaded by pandering illusions.

I recommend these qualities not to showcase our own goodness, which is radically flawed anyway, but to facilitate ministry. They cannot be successfully mimicked; only Christ can reproduce His life in us to the point where these traits are an unself-conscious part of who we are. Our obedience in these matters is a means to the worthwhile end of reaching kids.

THEIR ATTRIBUTES AND OUR MINISTRY

The flow and ebb of the cultural tidewaters thoroughly soak the younger generation. These fluctuating waves of influence alter the manner in which successive generations wander through adolescence. But there are certain characteristics of the adolescent period that will be expressed regardless of the momentarily fashionable mode of expression.

As youth ministers who mingle with young people, we need to be familiar with these characteristics (as well as with the currently approved outlets for their manifestation) and decide how to respond to them. I propose we accept the characteristics themselves as natural, normal (and even created), and morally neutral. They may easily drift in an unfortunate negative direction, but they may also be steered to a positive heading. The youth leader who cannot accept these characteristics, and who is threatened by them, may unknowingly push individuals toward a negative outcome. To ignore or stifle these traits is counterproductive. To affirm the trait and anticipate opportunities to channel it toward a healthy, even godly, fulfillment is the wisest approach.

Negative Drift	Neutral Characteristic	Positive Direction
1. disruptive	energetic	expressive
2. self-destructive	experimental	discovering
3. cynical/relativistic	testing beliefs; re-formulating values	mature
4. defiant/passive	challenging authority	critical responsiveness
5. anarchic	striving for independence	responsible
6. self-centered/ self-contemptuous	searching for identity	self-esteeming
7. demanding	impatient with process	assertive

8. self-indulgent	pleasure seeking	zestful
9. excluding/withdrawn	needing to belong	companionable
10. conforming	impressionable	teachable
11. solipsistic	introspective	honest sharing of feelings

The following list shows how a youth minister's awareness of and responses to the natural characteristics of adolescents can determine the success or failure of the ministry:

• To open a junior-high youth-group meeting with forty-five minutes of prayer is to invite trouble. Exuberant, rowdy interludes are essential in youth ministry. Teenagers are drawn to the new, the exciting, the unpredictable. Instead of always holding them back, by speaking in a tone that forbids and dampens, could we not entice and lead them into risky adventures of faith?

• In the middle of an earnest Bible study on Ephesians, a kid blurts out, "I think the church stinks!" Does he have a right to feel that way? Of course he does. Perhaps it is insolent, but it is not a threat to the secure youth leader.

"It sounds like you've had some bad experiences with the church. . . . I've had some problems with it myself. . . . What do you think the church is supposed to be like?" The youth leader who does not react defensively with a biting correction but acknowledges the strong feeling and then proceeds to enlist the discontented person as a partner in the search for a better way is likely to have a positive influence. For teenagers it is no longer good enough to parrot what they have been taught. It is time to make it their own (or overturn the heritage).

• The youth leader must be willing to undertake the burden of proof. If we are arbitrary in our authority, we will reap rebellion. If we resort to power plays, we can expect resistance.

- Teenagers want and need respect. They do not expect us to condone everything they do. To demonstrate our readiness to trust them with expanded roles, we should delegate the meaningful responsibilities they appear to be prepared to accept.
- Adolescents, especially, need a profusion of legitimate praise and support. It cannot be overdone, nor does it countermand needful exhortation. Sometimes, outrageous and offensive behavior is a veiled plea for attention. Many adults turn away in disgust or add to the abuse already absorbed.
- Today's teenager is like the youth in the ancient fable "The Emperor's New Clothes." Instead of complying with the vain hoax that the king was robed in the finest garments that could only be seen by those of true nobility (of course, no one could see the mythical wardrobe, but no one wanted to admit it), the youth exclaimed out loud, "The king is naked!" Yes, he is, quite often. And irreverent youth are not polite enough to refrain from making it known. If we can encourage frankness without promising to deliver on demand, we are teaching assertiveness.
- Christians can have great fun. We need to repossess the word "party" from the pagans and renew the idea of celebration with undisguised gusto.
- Providing a dynamic peer fellowship, all-inclusive and mutually reinforcing, is the awesome opportunity of a youth ministry. Never before and never again in their lives will adolescents have such an intense need to belong or so much time to spend or be so open.
- Teenagers are not yet set in their ways. But they are capable of understanding more than most adults realize. It is our mandate to expose them to the best.
- We can be a sounding board for young people who are sorting out their emotions. As we gently draw out and accept the effluence of their feelings, we are rendering a valuable service.

QUESTIONS

1. Which of Richard Niebuhr's four possible views of the relationship between Christ and culture characterizes your approach to ministry? Can you demonstrate that your view is consistent with your practice?

2. Would you go to a rock concert with kids? Argue both ways. Then defend your own decision.

3. What would be your approach in counseling a teenager whom you knew to be sexually active?

4. How would you rate yourself as a confronter of problem behavior based on the guidelines offered in the chapter? How could you improve?

5. Is there any area in which you exhibit a less than authentically Christian style of life? Does this affect your ministry?

6. Of the qualities that distinguish Christians as "stripped down" for youth ministry, where do you think you are strong? Where are you weak?

7. Do you agree that the "neutral characteristics" of adolescents listed on page 105 are realistic? If not, why are you uneasy about them?

8. Does your youth program honor these natural characteristics and attempt to direct them toward a positive fulfillment? Where are your problems? What do you need to do to correct them?

9. Do you understand the need to live within the paradox of being comfortable in our involvement with youth and, at the same time, being restless about situations we discover?

10. Can you offer an illustration of a ministry of "creative interference" that worked? And one that did not? Are the reasons for breakthrough and failure apparent to you?

PART II

YOUTH MINISTRY: MAKING IT HAPPEN

5 WHERE IS THE CHURCH?

At this point we need to discuss the nature of the church. Since the church carries out youth ministries, we must understand the form and mission of this mysterious entity that makes up the body of Christ Himself. To misunderstand its character is to miss the point of ministry.

Let us begin with several questions: Where does one go to find God? Where is the place of worship? Of fellowship? Of ministry? To answer these questions, we need to study the Bible.

HISTORICAL NOTES

The Old Testament patriarchs occasionally experienced theophanies, that is, phenomenal appearances of the Lord. Adam, Noah, Abraham, Isaac, Jacob, and Moses spoke to God and were privy to His plans and intentions. God was specifically working with these leaders to create a people for Himself.

After Moses spoke with God on Mount Sinai the Israelites were commanded to construct a portable tabernacle that would accompany them during their wilderness wanderings. A separate priesthood was established to administer the sacrificial rites. The high priest alone could enter the Holy of Holies that housed the sacred ark of the covenant. This inner sanctum of the tabernacle was recognized as the dwelling place of God with His people, though access was limited to one representative.

When the Hebrews occupied the land promised to their fathers and became a nation ruled by a king, the nomadic ritual of setting up and taking down the portable tabernacle was replaced by the institution of the temple. This magnificent building, constructed by Solomon on a hill called Zion in Jerusalem, incorporated many features of the tabernacle and contained many artifacts of the desert years. To worship the one true and living God, an individual had to go to this temple on Mount Zion; it was the physical center of Israel's existence. Even gentile proselytes were required to make a pilgrimage to the holy city.

After the destruction of Jerusalem and the temple in 587 B.C., the Jewish exiles, finding themselves in bondage in foreign countries, resorted to the synagogue as a small-scale substitute for the temple. The temple and its sacrifices, however, were irreplaceable; the rebuilding of this landmark by the returning Jews continued to be a high priority during these years. In time, the temple was rebuilt, although the synagogue continued to serve as an auxiliary temple for Jews living abroad. But the final destruction of the rebuilt temple in 70 A.D. by the Romans precipitated a perpetual crisis for the devout Jew.

While the temple was still standing in all of its glory, the prophesied Messiah was born. He was heralded as Emmanuel, "God with us." He alluded to Himself as "this temple" in such an emphatic way that the pious Jews who overheard His declaration mistook His bold claims as sedition (John 2:16–22). He was broadly hinting at a fact that was to shake the assumptions of not only first century Palestine but also most civilizations of the world for all subsequent time.

In Jesus, all the fullness of God dwells in bodily form (Colossians 2:9). "Anyone who has seen me has seen the Father" (John 14:9). With His public debut, the Kingdom of God is imminent (Matthew 4:17–25). The one sacrifice of Jesus for all people supercedes the Old Testament practice of animal sacrifice (Hebrews 9:6–26). He exercises authority to forgive sins (Mark 2:5–12). This series of jolting revelations, vindicated by the miracles and the Crucifixion and the unprecedented Resurrection, proclaim Jesus as the physical presence of God during His earthly career.

This tension between the figure of the Son of God and the

awe-inspiring temple surfaced in Jesus' conversation with the woman at the well (John 4). She wanted to know whether the Samaritans, who attend the site on Mount Gerizim, or their purebred rivals to the south in Judea were worshiping at the proper place. His response obviates this competition. Even the celebrated edifice in Jerusalem is on the verge of obsolescence. "Yet a time is coming and has now come when the true worshipers will worship the Father in spirit and truth" (v. 23). From that moment on, spiritual worship is not bound to a holy place but is mediated by the Truth—the One who fulfills God's covenant and proves Him to be trustworthy—which removes any lesser considerations.

Jesus Christ was the focus of worship while He was here. Anticipating His departure, He promised that the Father would impart the Holy Spirit to all who put their faith in the Son. At Pentecost that first community of believers received the Spirit in full measure.

The church, then, has been appointed as God's sanctified representative until Christ comes again. In a very real sense we are an extension of the Incarnation. The Christian's body is the true temple of the Holy Spirit (1 Corinthians 6:19). Corporately, we are being fitted like living stones into a spiritual building that has Christ as the cornerstone (1 Peter 2:4–8). The old ethnic, class, clerical, and sex distinctions no longer pertain to God's new creation, the universal church. We are the household of God, a holy temple in the Lord (Ephesians 2:19–22) and are members of the body of Christ (1 Corinthians 12:12–27). We are led to conclude that since the first, pivotal century God is to be found in His church.

A PROPER SELF-IMAGE FOR THE CHURCH

What are the implications of this teaching for the church today? Once again, the Scripture is clear, but our contemporary application is seriously confused, and our attempts at ministry suffer as a result.

The New Testament reminds us that the church is not a building. The notion of a holy place is out-of-date. The building

113

where the church gathers is not "the House of God" in any sense, and it is misleading to ascribe to this facility such a lofty significance. It is only brick and mortar—an expedient. The church is people.

If the church is not a static geographical location but a dynamic community of people, then we cannot speak meaningfully of coming or going to church, to a place. God does not inhabit the building; we do not visit Him on Sundays at His sacred quarters; the pastor is not the curator of the divine museum (see Acts 7:44–51). Rather, God by His Spirit lives in us; He is with us always—seven days a week. The pastor is an enabler of the ministering congregation.

The church, far from being a bastion of righteousness, a fortress that insulates its membership from the evil in the world, is called to be the church militant, a consort of commandos on the offensive, storming the gates of hell (Matthew 16:18). The urgency of this is lost on us much of the time. The following fictional conversation between Christ and His church portrays our reluctance to step into the arena:

I'll tell you a mystery.

Please, tell us, we like mysteries!

It is the mystery of a secret, hidden conflict.

It sounds exciting. Tell us more.

It is God's will that you understand the dimensions of this conflict.

Is this a real-life story or a fantasy?

It is very real and very contemporary.

Then I'm not sure we're interested.

There is a battle raging for the souls of men and women.

I'm certain this does not concern us. Why don't you pray about your problem?

You are the key participants in this war. The Lord is looking for a band of committed guerrilla fighters.

114

Tell Him to recruit in the seminaries.

You have already signed up, Christian. I have your orders.

You've got to be kidding. I don't have time, and I'm not really a leader. Besides, I don't see this battle you speak of.

Open your eyes to the needs of people around you. Admit your own vulnerability to attack. Feel the wounds you have already suffered.

We don't know what you're talking about. We're all right.

You don't know yourself very well. And you have lost touch with other people.

That's an insult.

That's right . . . but I still love you, and I still want your life to count.

Who are you?

You know me very well, but sometimes not at all. Follow me into my world. Trust me. I am telling you the truth. I want you to walk with me. I will show you how to do your part. The victory is ours. Just follow me. Are you coming?

To change the analogy, we are sojourners who should not get too attached to the shrines and monuments along the way. We are on the way to the New Jerusalem, our permanent home, where we will enjoy God together forever (Hebrews 11:8–16; Revelation 21:1–7, 22–23).

The real work of the church is in the world. As Christians, we are called to submerge ourselves in this world. The martyred bishop of El Salvador, Oscar Romero, remonstrated against the tendency toward introversion or neutrality:

> Our Salvadoran world is not an abstraction. It is a world which, in its vast majority, is composed of poor and oppressed men and women. We in the church have returned to the world of the poor and have found it to be our rightful place. Far from distancing us from our faith, its harsh realities have moved us to incarnate ourselves in the world of the poor.[1]

As the church, we gather together for worship and personal renewal, but then we are sent back out where the action is. Ian Thomas exhorts us to reclaim alien territory:

> I simply argue that the cross be raised again at the center of the marketplace as well as on the steeple of the church. I am recovering the claim that Jesus was not crucified in a cathedral between two candles but on a cross between two thieves, on the town garbage heap, at a crossroad so cosmopolitan that they had to write His title in Hebrew and in Latin and in Greek . . . at the kind of place where cynics talk smut and thieves curse and soldiers gamble. Because that is where He died, and that is what He died about. And that is where churchmen ought to be, and what churchmen should be about.[2]

Stan Mooneyham of World Vision rebukes our staid, sedentary terminology and mindset that immobilizes the church:

> The other day when I was reading about a certain church, I came upon the fact that it "seats 900." That's a common enough way of describing size. But, I wondered, is seating power the way a church should be measured? Wouldn't sending power be more relevant? I'd like to know if the church sends 900. Or even 90.
>
> Perhaps we've gotten in the habit of lumping churchgoing with spectator sports, where it is the coming and not the going that is important. That may help to explain why we attach such importance to glossy, fast-paced church services in which even the ushers are expected to perform with the choreographed precision of the Rockettes.
>
> The entertainment industry knows all about slickness and image, and if we are trying only to fill seats, that's probably the route. But it seems to me that the church might better be trying to empty its seats. The church is, or ought to be, a sending agency. A recruiting office doesn't talk about the number of recruits it can hold, but the number it has sent. Come to think of it, I have never seen a very big or a very plush recruiting office. They don't have to be, because the action is somewhere else.[3]

The *assembled* church and the *dispersed* church are both the church. But the *dismissed* church is in tragic disarray. Pastor-at-large Richard Halverson sees it this way:

The work of the church is what is done between Sundays when the church is scattered all over the metropolitan area where it is located—in homes, in schools, in offices, on construction jobs, in market places. This is the work of the church and it requires every single member. The responsibility of the pastor is to equip every member to do the work of the church wherever he is between Sundays.

One of the reasons the institutional church has become irrelevant to the extent that it has in our contemporary life is that many Christians have become so busy in church work they have not had time to do the work of the church. The religious establishment, the institution, the organization, the program demanded so much of their time they were not able to be the witness, the minister, the servant of God and man they were intended to be.

They were so involved in church work they were unable to be involved in the life of the larger community. The establishment preoccupied and preempted them. It is almost as if the church exists for itself. It is almost as if the important thing is the building and the program rather than the outreach into the world for which Christ died and to which God sent His church.[4]

The building is a convenience, and not even a necessary one. It is emphatically not sacred ground, nor are these "hallowed" halls worthy of reverential treatment. The mobile Body of Christ renders anachronistic all the hushed talk of temples, tabernacles, and houses of God. Instead of lingering behind four walls, we are challenged to emulate God's barrier-busting, boundary-extending, hell's-gate-crashing style of love.

The nature and composition of the church warn us away from the nominalism and formalism that sap our vitality. The Spirit is quenched when the process of institutionalization becomes self-serving; and ministry virtually ceases. All of this can happen while the organization hums, the numbers remain stable, and the income rises steadily. We may be lulled into believing that all is well. One wag observed that the three priorities of the typical church are _membership_ (euphemized as "helpers" and "giving units" who keep the machinery well oiled), _stewardship_ (the bottom line that keeps the ship afloat),

117

and *bullship* (all of the organizational propaganda and maneuvering necessary to insure loyalty and self-preservation). This is a crude caricature, but sadly, it is not far off the mark.

MOVING OUT

What does this mean for the church's youth ministry? As we move toward realigning the church with the pattern set by the Incarnation, our practice of youth ministry could be revolutionized. The following points deserve closer scrutiny:

- Youth ministry needs to be decentralized.
- Youth ministry should not be trapped inside the building.
- The building is not the church during the week, and it only shelters the church on those occasions the people congregate there.
- We do not need the building to commune with God; we are not closer to God there.
- The youth minister should not be confined to the building.
- The building and grounds should be evaluated in terms of their functional utility.
- Any activities appropriate for Christians can be held on the premises.
- We should attempt to demystify the sanctuary (and associated rooms) so that it becomes a place where kids can be themselves.
- The building itself should not be a cue for turning on artificial religious comportment (being quiet, for example).
- No special attire, vocabulary, posture, tone of voice, musical style or instrument, or furnishing can be reasonably cited as peculiar to this building.

I recognize that some or all of these points may be controversial. We may be afraid of losing something, of conceding too much, of being in danger of committing some modernist heresy. But I believe it is also heretical to absolutize our cultural preferences (teenagers always seem to lose the cultural battles in church). And as we loosen our grip on rules that only impede true ministry, we will be more attuned to the spiritual realities. The logic of this admittedly radical view of the church is compelling for those of us who are actively sifting the biblical record for clues. It is critical, however, that this view not be interpreted in a sectarian manner.

If we are not dependent on the facilities of the church, then we are free to shed our nearly idolatrous and suffocating allegiance to a building and to develop a much more flexible, penetrating, and even itinerant style of ministry. The facility may serve as a base of operations, but it must not become an enclosed citadel of retreat.

The question "Where do we go to find God?" can be asked in another way: "Where does genuine ministry take place?" The New Testament and much of church history answer simply and directly, "Anywhere and everywhere." It is not enough to invite people to church, that is, to the building; we must take the love of Christ to them. The difficulty of such an ambition should not be underestimated. *They* expect *us* to be *in church* and to limit the practice of our religion to that serene and secretive setting.

That ambition may also lead us into conflict, arousing the opposition of the guardians of our ecclesiastical traditions. Joseph Aldrich, educator and author, urges us to go out there despite the sniping. If we are to be "living epistles read of all men," we cannot be locked away.

> If you are pursuing lost sheep, you must go where they are. You cannot avoid every appearance of evil. Our Lord didn't either. Because of His close proximity to the beer cans and potato chips of His day He was accused of being a drunkard and a glutton. Professional "weaker brothers," suffering from hardening of the categories, delight to criticize those who take the Great Commission seriously.[5]

Christians in ministry (and they are the only kind who can carry the name) are pledged to infiltrate hostile territory. Here are some sites for significant youth ministry. This list only begins to suggest possibilities:

On campus
Extracurricular school activities

> In homes
> Hangouts/the streets/cruising/neighborhood gathering points
> Parks
> Beaches
> Playgrounds
> Amusement centers
> Fast-food restaurants
> Sporting events
> Parties
> Theaters
> Locker rooms
> Recreational clubs
> Concerts
> Slum areas/red-light districts/"combat zones"
> Juvenile detention centers
> Reform schools
> Prisons
> Hospitals
> Halfway houses/rehabilitation clinics
> Cult houses and meetings
> Crisis situations/disaster areas
> Community meetings
> Camps/resorts/wilderness areas
> Church facilities

Can ministry really be done effectively in such unlikely places? Is this the role of the church? It can, is, and must be done; and the local church is the ideal choice for the assignment. This is true even though we must recognize that it is the parachurch groups that have led the way and still fill the empty spaces abandoned or ignored by the church.

ON CAMPUS

This aggressive strategy is illustrated by examining the possibilities for ministry on the public secondary-school campuses. You will notice that I have not begun to talk about starting up the youth program at the church's facilities. We will get to that. It is so easy to get attached to the building that an emphasis on ministry away from the building may be a bracing corrective to the usual practice. There is a strong temptation, reinforced by tradition, to sit in a comfortable office, creating a marvelous paper ministry that, as it turns out, is oblivious to the turmoil in the world outside.

When I was a volunteer club leader with Young Life during my last two years of college, I was introduced to the idea of *contact work*—going where the kids are to "earn the right to be heard." I bought the idea, but I could not overcome my inhibitions about taking the plunge. I was not emotionally ready, so the concept lay dormant for a time.

Several years later, going to the campuses to mingle with students at school-related events had become one of the most fulfilling aspects of my youth ministry. Getting on campus was something I looked forward to and hated to miss.

The key is breaking in. A few recommendations might help to clear the initial hurdles. First, the youth leader must be committed to a consistent involvement that is frequent enough to ensure recognition and continuity. Showing up every other month qualifies us as strangers. Any cheating on this commitment will erode both our motivation and our accomplishments.

Second, we must assume the burden of proving to the school authorities that we are an asset to them. They have an important responsibility to limit access to the property. Somehow, we have to convince the administration that we care about their school, that we are there to affirm and support the students we already know and to extend genuine friendship to their friends, and that we are not there to proselytize or hustle kids for our program. It is better to let kids invite other kids to our activities.

In these tight-budget days, schools are usually open to accepting responsible volunteers for their programs. Assisting with sports, music, drama, social events, tutorial help, counseling, being a guest speaker in class, or being available to respond to chronic problems (such as racial strife, drug abuse, vandalism) are all ways to gain entrance. If the staff comes to trust us, many more doors will swing open.

Third, as we overcome the psychological and institutional barriers, we need to sternly remind ourselves why we are there. We seek visibility without ostentation, proximity without intrusion, and credibility without coercion. We are there to encourage the teenagers who are Christians—to build their confidence in the knowledge that Christ walks their campus and bids them to share His love with others. We are also anxious to meet their friends and undermine any misconceptions about Christians and Christianity that keep them away from official church services in droves. "Who are these guys, anyway?" they will ask. Their curiosity about us can work to our advantage.

It is imperative that we "connect" with their agenda. I have often been unimpressed with the results of Bible studies and prayer sessions held on campus, especially if they are flaunted as evangelistic forays into the schools. Behind-the-scenes fellowship (such as a before-school prayer breakfast), on the other hand, can be a source of strength for believers. Passing out leaflets or other "cold" hit-and-run approaches are almost never as meaningful as the time-consuming effort to develop authentic relationships.

IN CONCLUSION

Review these recommendations in light of the fundamental principles of incarnational ministry as detailed in the previous section. If they do not line up, we are not operating within our professed philosophy of ministry. That realization should shake us and cause us to recalculate our strategy.

When we hit a snag in ministry, we must recall our original model. The problem is either our inability to assimilate and express the injunctions of the model or—and we should be cognizant of this possibility—that our faithfulness has incurred the retaliation of those forces that do not appreciate the distinctive ambience of agape.

Wherever young people are, the church should be there. Where there is trouble, where there are needs, where Christians are not expected—that is where we should be. "What are you doing here?" is the question that, when it is asked of us, confirms that we are in the right place.

The only thing unusual about our presence ought to be the

startling fact that we care—that single attribute can make all the difference in the world. There is a shortage of active concern these days, particularly in the nether world of teenagers. Youth ministry that does not take to the turf of young people and meet them on their terms is enfeebled. If the ministry fails to produce an effect beyond the holy days and sacred spots, it is not even halfway there. Snapping out of our myopic trance restores the vistas of the church's worldwide ministry.

Christ has gone before us, and we have been enlisted to follow Him. We have our marching orders.

QUESTIONS

1. Where is the dwelling place of God today? Trace the history of God's presence throughout Scripture.

2. Is it important to be semantically accurate in identifying the church? Why or why not? Is the church a place?

3. How does formal institutionalization threaten youth ministry?

4. How can you decentralize youth ministry? What is gained by doing so? What might be lost?

5. How can youth leaders communicate this vision of the church to the church at large? Can you anticipate the objections of the opposing forces?

6. Is any place off-limits to your youth ministry at this time? Are the reasons clear?

7. Which sites on the list (pp. 119–20) have been penetrated by your ministry and which have not? Brainstorm possible locations and consider tactical approaches to them.

8. Could you find a way to gain access to campus activities, or are you convinced that it is not possible? What personal fears do you have about mingling on adolescents' own turf?

9. What happens, philosophically, if you feel a particular avenue is closed and yet is mandated by the incarnational pattern of ministry? How can such dilemmas be resolved?

10. How do you think the kids in your group feel when they see you mingling in their activities? What might the benefits be?

6 CONNECTIONS

RELATIONAL DYNAMICS

Youth ministry sets up a range of personal encounters. These "connections" are the medium of communication for Christ's love. Without paying careful attention to the cultivation of significant relationships, such communication is blocked or seems contrived.

How do we establish these connections? In a variety of ways, from the informal to the formal, and in a diversity of contexts. And we are required to increase our awareness of situations and methods through which we can creatively make contact with people. There are many pitfalls along the way, and the great sensitivity required to avoid them may explain why so few adults can communicate comfortably and meaningfully with teenagers. A language barrier seems to be in place.

It is a constant struggle to personalize our ministry, to press for deeper relationships. Not only is it arduous and even exhausting for an adult to reach out to teenagers, but the risks are considerable. To keep our distance, to produce a show for the kids, to package a ministry by means of a patented formula—all of these "justifiable" tactics in ministry protect us from the uncontrollable complications of a truly relational style.

Honest relationships allow others to see us as we are; we become vulnerable. We may squirm at the prospect of no longer hiding behind our cool façades.

But transparency need not be exhibitionism if we are moved by God's love. Intimacy is both compelled and restrained by a higher consideration. As Dietrich Bonhoeffer described it, our relationships are mediated by Christ. He is the bond of friendship that exists between people. Since He stands between us, we do not have immediate access to each other, and anyone who wants to possess, impress, or enforce his or her will upon another is doing the work of the devil. Christ asks us to serve one another for His sake.[1]

No matter how close I come to you, you are not *mine* but always *His*. That fundamental recognition reminds me to respect your inviolable dignity and your best interests, and it prevents me from exploiting you. I find it is distressing that we must take time to distinguish youth ministry from its reprehensible counterfeits—empire building, spiritualized manipulation, pedophilia. We must be absolutely clear in our motives.

Adolescents want and need attention—the right kind of attention from the right people. How do we respond to this unspoken need? We are off to a good start when we learn and remember their names and when we relate to them on a mutual first-name basis. This, in itself, invites them to be at ease with us.

Unilaterally, we need to express a sincere interest in the young person; we communicate this by our body language and friendly demeanor. Rarely will an adolescent respond in kind at first, although he or she will be surreptitiously checking us out. We should not be put off by the absence of any response, but we should trust that our friendliness has registered. It may not be until much later that the value of our overtures will be confirmed.

In our attempt to convince young people of our warm regard, we need to listen to them. Their parents shut them off; other adults talk at them; and their peers vie for center stage. We must listen sympathetically. Asking questions will give us the opportunity to listen, and as we listen we can empathize with their feelings. We should suspend judgment on any dubious revelations until we understand the history and circumstances.

By spending time with kids and doing ordinary things together, we build a framework for ministry. In the process, some (though not all) will come to esteem us as solid friends who are worthy of trust.

The following ideas suggest opportunities to deepen relationships and to share concerns:

> Go with someone to a school athletic event.
> Take the person along on one of your errands (driving time in a car facilitates conversation).
> Meet the person at his or her house.
> Go bowling.
> Play miniature golf.
> Go to a worthwhile movie.
> Go to the beach or lake.
> Go out to dinner.
> Go out for ice cream.
> Go to his or her house or your house and work on or fix something.
> Loan them a good Christian book or album and discuss it later.
> Put in a casual telephone call.
> Attend a school play.
> Attend a concert (Christian or otherwise).
> Take a small group skiing.
> Drive a kid home after school.
> Watch a television show together.
> Arrange to meet someone during the lunch hour.
> Drive a kid home after a youth-group event.
> Meet for breakfast before school.
> Have a girls' slumber party or a guys' overnight.
> Help a person with his or her homework.
> Write a letter, note, or card.
> After you attend an activity together, go for something to eat or drink on the way home (more time to talk).
> Play games like ping-pong, basketball, chess, etc.
> Take a walk or go hiking.
> Play a game.
> Drop by with one of their friends.

We can set it up by:

> Procuring a roster of the youth group.
> Making a note to yourself of kids to see and call.
> Calling them up.
> Making an appointment at the youth-group meeting, on

Sundays, etc.
Volunteering to pick them up.
Asking their good friends to bring them.
Calling to confirm just ahead of time.

We need to be available, and we need to be people who can be interrupted. If we are tied up when someone wants to see us, we should always make an appointment for the near future. We do not want to parcel out slim tokens of our attention. We should be prepared to give them as much time and attentiveness as they need.

But such radical openness could overwhelm us. Perhaps three considerations will help to relieve some of the tension. First, we will have to resort to a team approach. The capacity of each of us is limited. In my opinion a youth group should not exceed a maximum of ten youth for every adult leader. Second, God can expand our capacity for relational breadth and depth. As He quiets our fears and insecurities, we are liberated to be absorbed with the needs of others without wasting time shoring up our defenses. Third, experience has taught me that my Lord will send just the right number of crises across my path. It is never more than He and I can handle.

I am convinced that we need to learn much more about love. It is not an overstatement to allege that we could key our whole theology to this cogent theme. Love never takes advantage of another, does not keep a record of wrongs, does not insist on its own way, and does not demand rights and recognition. Love is kind, accepting, and hangs in there (1 Corinthians 13). Love dictates wisdom to the youth leader who is tempted to compete, ignore, exploit, or give up. This love, demonstrated so forcefully by Jesus Christ and spelled out in the Word, is an adequate guide for us in our ministry. How easily we get sidetracked.

Love is not a means to an end—love is the end. Young people need to be loved for their own sakes, not because they are prospective converts. Love with conditions is not love. Our unmitigated love for young people is in itself the most powerful witness to the gospel that we hope they will embrace.

Our perception of the task at hand will determine the quality of the relationships we enter into. A recent article clarified this disjunction between "soul winning" and "soul caring":

> It seems to me that "winning" is a self-directed concept. Caring is an other-directed concept. To win, you have to come in ahead of someone else. You are in competition. Remember this gospel song: "Will there be any stars in my crown?" I never thought of those "stars" as human beings in their own right. I saw them as decorations for me. I'd like to see the word "trophy" dropped from our evangelistic vocabulary, too. The word gives me the mental image of the heads of wild animals mounted in somebody's den, and I want to be more than a display for some spiritual big-game hunter. . . .
>
> Soul-winning, as we commonly use the expression, often deals in numbers, fostering the impression that evangelicals are interested primarily in spiritual body counts or in completing a somewhat burdensome assignment with as little inconvenience as possible. We're not doing much thinking—or caring—about the earthly environment to which saved souls will have to return and in which they are expected to operate happily and victoriously with little further attention from us. . . .
>
> If "winning" is all we are interested in, maybe we deserve what we are not getting. If we want to "win" without moving close to the lost one, without touching him, without sharing something of his life and hope and hurt, without venturing into his lostness, without trying to make him a friend before making him a convert (and not simply to make him a convert), we're going in the wrong direction, whatever the assistance of how-to seminars, computers and communication gimmicks.[2]

God's love has a way of disrupting our petty schemes as well as our flowery evasions. The reductionism of love speaks in unambiguous terms, forcing us to declare our intentions. Love would say:

You are of infinite value to me.

It is you, and not certain qualities about you

129

or possessions you have
that I am unconditionally committed to.

My commitment to you is not limited or modified
by your imperfections.

My decision to love you means that I will actively endeavor
to do you good.

I hope that you will love me too,
but my attitude toward you
is not dependent upon your response.

I love you because God created you in His image
and sent His Son to redeem you in order
to make you a whole, beautiful person.

I am commanded to extend myself to you
in the same way.

I can love you because God first loved me
and has given me His divine love for you.

I want you to understand that I really love you!

The great irony of youth ministry is that although we are called to spend ourselves in service to young people, we are supposed to relax in the assurance that God will work through us, and in spite of us, to accomplish His purposes. An uptight, perfectionistic youth leader drives people away. In our attempt to make sure it all works out, we sometimes become overbearing. Soon we will find ourselves patronizing the teenagers and stifling relationships.

The following list of "Youth Club" members' responsibilities was handed out to a senior-high group at a church. Think about the subtle messages conveyed by this list.

1. To be on time every week and to stay for the entire program.
2. To participate in all aspects of the Youth Club program, i.e., crafts, singing, games, study, service, dinner, vespers. To participate in the extra activities if I am able to do so.

3. To observe good manners and seemly conduct at all times.

4. To show respect for the church building and program supplies.

5. To clear away my place at the dinner table and return to the table until I am excused by an adult.

6. To clean the dining room when my table is assigned that job.

7. To show respect for all adults and teachers present and to try to get to know them as my friends.

8. To try to be a special friend to all other Youth Club members—"We are one in the Spirit, we are one in the Lord . . . And they'll know we are Christians by our love."

9. To share our faith with our friends inside and outside the church and bring them as guests to Youth Club. Guests come one week for free. Members are responsible for their guests. Be sure to tell them what to do and introduce them to others.

AGREEMENT

We, the _____ family have read this page of instructions and understand what is expected of both parents and the members of Youth Club and feel that we are ready and willing to make the spiritual, financial, and physical commitment necessary to be part of this program.

Member's signature   Parent's signature

I cannot decide whether this list of requirements would be more appropriate for a junior scout troop or a juvenile detention center. The tone is offensively condescending. It displays not even the barest appreciation for the special sensitivities of teenagers. Rules three, four, and five are particularly galling— as if little children were being addressed. And rule seven poses an impossible contradiction: a demand for a show of respect in conjunction with an invitation to warmth and closeness. Good luck! If the damage to morale were not so serious, this list would read like a satire.

PRINCIPLES OF COMMUNICATION

Most American teenagers speak English. But it is usually an idiomatic variation that nearly qualifies as a distinct dialect. Their language may be characterized as follows:

Visceral. It is raw, gutsy, aggressive, emotional, and loud. It communicates imprecisely what the person feels.

Earthy. It is not abstract or subtle. It is concerned with the here and now and will express itself in uncensored form. Polite euphemisms are not substituted for the inelegant, often pungent, observation.

Hyperbolic. Deliberate exaggeration is used for effect.

Informal. It is casual, careless about correct grammar, and not intended to be taken with total seriousness. An assertion may be tentatively offered but quickly withdrawn, as if to say "don't hold me to it".

Abbreviated. It delivers chopped, terse expressions with an economy of syllables. A teenager makes points quickly without wasting words.

Coded. It is purposely obscured to exclude unwanted adults and other aliens; if a term (*cop out,* for instance) is co-opted by outsiders, it will be dropped from their lexicon.

Profane. Disrespectful phrasings and obscene expletives make for a kind of verbal swagger, warning away the squeamish.

Trendy. The latest fad contributes its own coinages to the vocabulary. Adaptations of the "in" words can result in unconventional syntax.

All youth leaders should be bilingual—fluent in the latest usage. This familiarity will have an influence on our style of communication in both the informal setting and the structured program.

We need to rethink our approach. Most kids have heard very little in church that makes sense to them. Even our Sunday schools, catechisms, and youth programs transmit a largely irrelevant ritual that inspires a synchronization of cavernous yawns.

The opportunity to speak to a group of teenagers should be taken seriously. The challenge to close the distance between us is sobering, but the chance to reverse the inertia and propose life-changing options presents us with an exciting and propitious opportunity. As we prepare to share ourselves and the Word with them, there are a number of considerations we ought to be mindful of:

- We would do well to forget the sleep-inducing preaching style we are accustomed to when the church congregates. To reproduce the tone of drone could have fatal consequences for our ministry.
- We must always translate theological concepts into the vernacular. Linguists refer to this reformulation as *dynamic equivalence*. To retrieve the essential meaning for our audience, we must sensitively and creatively change the form of expression.
- We need to develop a colorful repertoire of stories that touch their experience. The gift of storytelling is to be cultivated.
- We will want to generously and naturally inject humor into our talk. This does not mean that a youth speaker must be a flamboyant comedian. Sometimes that is overdone and sabotages the central theme. But a dry, humorless presentation will not win a hearing.
- It is advisable to illustrate extravagantly from all sorts of sources, particularly ones with which they are familiar. Every abstract truth needs an example to help people picture it. Otherwise the truth remains suspended in the clouds.
- We should tell about the extraordinary in the context of the ordinary. We need to avoid pretentious and mystical presentations. Instead, the most abstract concepts must be put into the context of their world.
- Predictability is the bane of the youth speaker. If adolescents think they know where we are going, they will not listen. The brain goes on automatic pilot. To surprise them with twists and turns of the plot is to hold their interest.
- It is a grave error to talk too long when speaking to a youth group. Of course, the more interesting we are, the lower the risk. But there is a point of diminishing returns, and we must not presume upon their attention span. For example, I think that speaking more than twenty or possibly twenty-five minutes to high-school kids, without a break, is stretching the

133

limit. It is far better to stimulate their appetite for more than to provoke them into daydreaming of ways to shut us off.
- We should carefully analyze the physical setting in advance. Is it comfortable? Can the speaker take charge?
- Finally, youth leaders who address groups of young people have permission to be themselves. The catch is, most of us are not ourselves when we speak in front of a group. We must work on the technical speech difficulties that distort what we intend to express. Nervousness is the dreaded enemy. However, it is futile to fight the rush of adrenaline; it is more constructive to let that burst of energy animate our voices, gestures, and our appeal to the audience.

Good communication is dialogue, never a performance. Listening to teenagers is the best preparation for speaking to them. If we have listened to them, we reap their positive regard, which inclines them to be open to our comments. As we eavesdrop on their world, we know them at a deeper level and can better accommodate their interests and moods. As we listen, we silently test their reaction to our message. We broaden our own range of feelings as we study the experience of these adolescents.

Too many Christian youth leaders have stopped listening. If they cannot be in control and be the one everyone else is submissively listening to, they are not content. After a while they end up talking to themselves and resenting the inattention displayed by those "immature teenagers." To be enamored of the sound of one's own voice is a cardinal failing.

THE SECULAR AUDIENCE
Too many times we assume that the world is not interested in spiritual matters. If we mean that they do not always respond positively to evangelistic rhetoric, then we are right. Yet humankind is incurably religious and inquisitive about the transcendent meaning of the past, present, and future. That restlessness cannot be satisfied by the trinkets now being hawked as panaceas in our society. If we are confident that the

incarnate truth will quench the insatiable thirst of a parched world, we will not hesitate to take our turn on any available platform.

Youth workers who cruise the corridors of the youth culture discover ever-increasing opportunities to meet with and speak to teenagers, their parents, and other adults engaged in youth-related work. How do we take advantage of this exposure when it is offered to us at a school, club, or community activity?

We should select a topic that intersects the interests of the audience. Dealing with such subjects as drugs, racism, music, human relations, literature, sexuality, communications, and others in which the speaker might have some expertise is promising.

Actually, I have found that an overtly religious topic presents the most difficulty in a secular setting. The defense mechanisms of an adolescent audience are firmly in place whenever a speaker is tagged as "one of those." Nevertheless, I try not to turn down any chance to speak. Virtually any opportunity can be redeemed. Once, to my dismay, one of our senior-high student leaders volunteered me for a debate with a Ph.D. biologist on the topic "creation versus evolution" to be held on consecutive days in front of several combined science classes. The debate may have been a draw, but a draw is usually a moral victory for the underdog. I had one major advantage in understanding teenagers better than my opponent. In the end, it was a very enjoyable experience.

If the youth leader is asked to be a guest speaker for youth in a constitutionally "clean" environment, that is, an environment (such as public schools) in which civil jurisdiction forbids religious indoctrination, the following guidelines will be helpful:

- As always, speak their language, and purge your statements of all religious jargon.
- Start with, and continue to speak to, their concerns.
- Since Christians are just about the only real humanists left, we must demonstrate our high estimate of people—one that does not get lost on the theoretical level. Picking up on names,

personalities, and unique characteristics of the various individuals and factions present, paying attention to the fringes of the crowd, and establishing human contact all help to heighten interest.

- The emotional overtones of controversial issues can be explored profitably and can become a means of drawing in the audience.
- A message that balances realism and hope (hinting at a transcendent source) will leave a strong impression with the listeners.
- A gracious, no-holds-barred attitude toward audience participation (interruptions, ad libs, light repartee) will prove disarming.
- To clinch the discussion, we can extend a challenge that prevents us from merely indulging our audience (playing to the youth, for example) or acting as an onerous adult authority figure. The challenge is made in a personal way and infers a moral and even spiritual dimension to our lives. Pre-evangelistic hints of *the* answer, interjected in an incidental manner, are appropriate if they are not contrived like commercial messages. Our sense of discretion in this neutral setting is not to be confused with coyness. If someone asks a direct question, we should not duck it. It is hoped that such an occasion will reap the benefits of follow-up conversations and a greater openness to Christianity.

THE EVANGELISTIC SETTING

After defining the audience and what is appropriate to it, consideration must be given to the evangelistic setting. Here our prudence should define the perimeters. Many of the guidelines already outlined pertain; but in our own youth program, we are able to go further.

If we are attracting teenagers who have not yet come to faith, then we are presented with the evangelistic opportunity. The evangelistic message, of course, is only one factor among many that influence a young person's response to Jesus Christ.

But that message, complemented and sustained by an atmosphere rich in affection, can elicit a favorable response.

We can assume that we need to "melt" their defenses. After all, they probably have some very good and strongly felt reasons for not being committed. Strive to identify with their experience. It is not *you* but *we* that have problems, hurts, fears, and dreams. These should be portrayed strikingly but sympathetically.

Again, we must discipline ourselves to paraphrase and eliminate "church talk." The vernacular is the language God speaks—we do believe in plain revelation, don't we? Our presentations should be contemporary and dramatic, engaging our listeners in an impelling sequence of thought that progresses to the gospel punch line.

It is unfair to demand a blind leap of faith. We need to offer convincing reasons, not simply claims and assertions. We must be aware of their counterarguments (their intellectual objections), the dynamics of their situation within a particular environment (their cultural resistance), and the painful realities of their lives (their emotional resistance).

We need to show them that the Christian life works while at the same time we are appealing for a recognition of its validity. The epistemology of adolescents requires us to work both sides at once. Above all, it is incumbent upon the youth speaker to reveal how Jesus Christ fulfills all of our legitimate human longings and aspirations (though in a more profound way than we had imagined).

The person and work of Christ is the central reality of our message. We will get sidetracked if we initiate debates on secondary issues (such as, was Jonah really swallowed by a whale or which mode of baptism is correct). We also have to be careful about attacking other viewpoints (such as saying that the Mormons are out-to-lunch or Buddhism is laughable). We should always respect people, even while we undermine their position.

There are many ways to close an outreach meeting. No matter which method we choose, extreme caution and sensitivity must be exercised. If our youth ministry is developed to the extent that we host a regular (weekly) outreach activity allowing ongoing personal contact, we should recognize that the messages (and other input) have a cumulative effect. Nevertheless, we need to improvise a plan for the harvest. This list of alternative closings could be used on a selective basis:

- Leave it hanging—end without resolution.
- Close with a song, a reading, a dramatic scenario.
- Leave them with a provocative question to ponder.
- Designate a place for them to talk with the speaker afterward.
- Follow up with small discussion groups.
- Ask them to fill out a brief questionnaire.
- Ask them to write down questions or comments (such as "What doubts or problems still stand in the way of your becoming a full-time Christian?").
- Follow up with a personal visit.

Direct methods of soliciting a decision include:

- Raising hands.
- Standing.
- Coming forward (followed by personal counseling and distribution of literature).
- Looking up while everyone else is in prayer (a lower key yet direct confrontation by eye contact).

There is a law of diminishing returns with any method that is repeated. The problem with not using any method of closing is that the teenagers may not know what their response is supposed to be—or that they should respond. It is hard to underestimate the apathy that hangs like a pall over adolescent society. Ideally, an effort should be made to maintain a low leaders-to-kids ratio to assure that comprehensive, personalized follow-up is provided.

Young people have the right to say that they are not ready to make a decision—that they need more time and information. They have a right not to be pushed or emotionally wrung out. They also have a right to say no (a terrible right!). In either instance we cannot withdraw our love or attention. It is heartbreaking to watch a young person back away from the brink of new life. But it is the individual's decision, and cajoling or bribery is inappropriate. We should heed the warning that an indignant commentator directed at the "fundamentalist" style of evangelism:

> "If you died tonight, would you go to heaven or Hell?" This question (an all-out assault, really) smacks of spiritual terrorism. In the electronic church versions, spiritual terrorism is combined with material pandering. "Here's what Jesus did for me. Give Him a try and see what He'll do for you." Jesus pays off. In cash, business success, in happy homes, in sexual satisfaction, in whatever currency you're in the market for. Following a recent testimonial from a squeaky-clean, ebullient young actress, the MC turns to the camera and says, "you too can have that Jesus glitter."
>
> Very positive, but having little to do with the Jesus of history and the Christian faith. Note that Jesus seldom appears in these programs. He is not even talked about very much. Jesus does not sell well. What sells well is what Jesus can do for you. An old (church) axiom says to know Christ is to know His benefits. The TV version turns that into knowing Christ in order to get His benefits. Or, more precisely, in order to get our benefits. And, of course, running through the sales pitch is the not-so-veiled threat that, "if you don't accept Jesus, God's going to get you."
>
> We are told that without such pandering and terrorism, evangelism goes limp. Evangelistic hype-men do it the way God would have done it, had He known better. But God didn't do it their way, and He doesn't now. His way is unqualified and all-encompassing love. Love has no backstop. It risks all. Love has no pay-off. It is its own reason for being.[3]

Love energizes the reluctant evangelist and restrains the overzealous soul stalker. But evangelism must always be placed in a relational context or else it is in danger of becoming hollow rhetoric.

THE DISCIPLING VENUE

Communicating with young Christians is a privilege that should be highly regarded by the youth minister. There needs to be a regular time and place for nurturing those who have taken the first steps toward Christ. There is so much we can share together. We can encourage them to:

• Acquire an appetite to go deeper and further in their relationship with Christ.
• Integrate Scriptural views and precepts into their lives.
• Rely on Jesus in all circumstances as a close friend.
• Sense the reality of complete forgiveness.
• Clarify misunderstandings about doctrinal and moral issues.
• Develop self-discipline in devotional practice and personal habits.
• To be "real" with their Christian brothers and sisters.
• To reach out to their non-Christian friends.
• To work out conflicts with family members.
• To affirm their own worth, dignity, and beauty in Christ.

These are the means of building up those who have trusted Christ. In general, we should refrain from giving them the impression that:

• Jesus is only a means to our own selfish ends.
• We, as leaders, sit in self-righteous judgment on their behavior.
• The Christian life is all sunshine and smiles.
• Absorbing the biblical data is the goal of discipleship.
• Spirituality is relegated to a separate time and place.

The youth leader should still practice the sound principles of communication when speaking to the more advanced in spiritual maturity. The "pious persona" should not take over. We often tend to become more somber when we gather for Bible study. We also tend to go longer, as if Christian kids do not get impatient and weary from overlong sessions with the flavor left out.

The advantages of this setting are significant. We can

experience greater depth, more discussion, a more personal focus, some degree of accountability, the fellowship of prayer, worshipful singing, more intimate expressions of affirmation, and a fuller appreciation of God's Word.

The following representation summarizes the variable settings we have considered:

Setting	Nature of Message	Audience Focus	Target	Goal
secular	pre-evangelism	speaker	non-Christians	positive association; create openness
evangelistic	decision-oriented	speaker and Christ	non-Christians and Christians	challenge to consider and trust Christ
discipling	edification	speaker and Christ and others	Christians	nurture; to live more for Him

A footnote on the stark designation "non-Christian" is in order. Ultimately, as in the C.S. Lewis allegory, there is a "great divorce."[4] Each person's choice to respond to God's love as revealed in Jesus Christ or to turn away from Him has eternal consequences. Finally, after pursuing us at an exorbitant cost to Himself, God will honor our wishes. But we in the ministry must reserve the right of that determination for the Judge who knows the heart. We can only clarify the alternatives. I think it is preferable to let the kids eventually tell us where they stand and to accept their self-description at face value. I like to refer to those young people who are still outside the church as "not-yet-Christians" (or as "still on the way"). This is a signal of hope and a reflection of that divine passion for all to come to salvation. In any case, we should be wary of taking it upon ourselves to assign spiritual status to individuals.

THE DISCUSSION CIRCLE

Interaction is more difficult to control than monologue. The lecture is a linear mode of communication; we can predetermine our destination. The kids cannot throw us off with interruptions and digressions. There is a place for the monologue—the one-way talk. But it is no doubt overused. We need to engage young people, and that means we must open up the important topics for discussion and accept the risks that are entailed.

Unfortunately, what is billed as discussion too often turns into an excuse for a lecture by the innocently conniving or nervous leader, much to the consternation of the participants who were led to expect something much more open-ended. To assist a fruitful discussion that is not a sermon in disguise nor a discursive bull session, the adult discussion leader could benefit from this advice:

- Get everyone talking early. Start with an easygoing, ice-breaker topic or question to which everyone has a reaction.
- Keep the conversation at their level of interest and experience.
- Cultivate the fine art of asking questions and devising follow-up questions. Do not take over if it stagnates—spend more time with the nonthreatening, generalized icebreaker.
- Do not answer your own question—leave it unresolved for a while. Do not permit closure with a pious cliché.
- Ask for examples of the opinions they hold; keep them honest.
- Accept all statements without compulsively editorializing.
- Toss in current illustrations of the positions and problems that have surfaced.
- Be personal and vulnerable.
- Guide the group toward a consensus based on biblical principle and syllogism comprehensible to the adolescent mindset.
- Be sensitive to the tone and body language of each person. Never forfeit the battle (that individual's good will) to win the skirmish (disregarding the person to establish a technical point). Follow up the group period with appropriate individual contact.

We need to be thoroughly prepared, but secure enough to keep it loose and fun. Even intense discipleship cells should not lose the give-and-take dynamic. Conscientious planning and intelligent, though not dominant, direction can facilitate an invigorating experience. Obviously, leading a discussion is not a mechanical skill but an art form that requires hours of preparation and practice.

PUTTING IT TOGETHER

Few adults communicate effectively with teenagers. At the same time, I believe that most youth leaders could develop into speakers who connect. Brilliant oratory is not the key. The following criteria should be used to facilitate lively communication:

- Select a theme that suits the goals of the program and is (or could be) a matter of concern to the young people in the audience.
- Arrange a simple outline that explains a single, significant point.
- Illustrate every concept.
- Keep it moving; ruthlessly eliminate filler; know where you are going; and lead them to the climax.
- Rehearse and revise the talk, anticipating the responses of the listeners.
- Speak with a minimum of notes.
- Speak directly and personally in a colloquial manner.
- Speak with conviction and integrity, without even a trace of self-importance.
- Enjoy the time with them, and freely express the affective content of the theme, as well as the objective and intellectual.
- Time the message in advance so that it does not run too long.
- Solicit feedback from your most reliable critics, both the tough ones and the supportive ones.

MEDIA OPTIONS

The spoken word delivered in person is still indispensable to ministry. But media should be used to supplement this primary channel. Developing a variety of techniques and forms of communication will greatly enhance the palatability of the message.

The youth minister should gain access to media resources and invent a convenient system for their use. It will be worth our energy and time to muster all the creativity we can in this effort. Exploring leads and browsing through lists and catalogs are advised. Are there ways to integrate these other modes into our overall program design without disrupting the flow? (Does our program really flow, or is it better known for its slug- gishness?) Diversions into creative tributaries can be rejuvenat- ing. Consider the following:

- *Film:* feature-length, shorts, clips, slides.
- *Music:* live, recorded, lyrics.
- *Drama:* skits, scenes, readings, characterizations.
- *Props:* visual aids, sketches, artwork, posters.
- *Multiple Speakers:* panel, debate, open forum.
- *Guest Speaker:* Be selective; it is a mistake for any youth leader to speak too frequently—our effectiveness will become diluted.

We should not overuse any single medium, nor should we hesitate to consider new alternatives. To lapse into a dull, repetitive routine is inexcusable.

QUESTIONS

1. Why is a truly relational style of youth ministry more complicated? How do you feel when conversations and situations are unpredictable and uncontrollable?

2. How can we avoid possessiveness in youth ministry?

3. Are you comfortable relating on a mutual first-name basis with fifteen-year-olds?

4. Are you a good listener? Do kids think you are?

5. Do you like to spend time with kids? Are you becoming more patient and accepting of manifestations that once aggravated you?

6. What is the difference between soul winning and soul caring? Do you care about them? How do they know?

7. What impressions are created by the list of the Youth Club members' responsibilities? Put yourself in the kids' place.

8. Can you talk teenage? Can you translate it?

9. How can you improve your communication skills? Are you willing to work at it?

10. How do you feel about speaking to a mixed audience of Christians and non-Christians? How could you grow in your ability and confidence?

11. What is the best way to ask young people to make a spiritual decision? How is it best followed up?

12. Do you have experience in discipling young people? Have the results been similar to the opportunities presented in the chapter?

13. How do you feel about yourself as a discussion leader? Which of the items in the list on page 142 challenges you?

14. If you have not done so, carefully follow the steps suggested for putting together a message and see if the result is any different. What do you think could happen?

15. Are you familiar with media options? Do you agree that they could be profitably used in your youth programs? What resources do you have?

7 DESIGN AND MANAGEMENT

I have deliberately resisted specifying the kind of program a carefully developed philosophy of ministry might produce. But eventually, our convictions must result in concrete activities. There are many good how-to books in the field, and it is not my intention to add to that helpful collection but instead to explore the sources that give substance to the visible operation. I enjoy the creative challenges of programming, but it is not in the exchange of program ideas that we come to understand the nature of ministry.

Our approach generates the program. There is no ideal arrangement. The foregoing review and evaluation of the fundamentals of youth ministry should have instilled confidence and a sharper multidimensional vision into those of us who tend to get preoccupied with skimming the magazines, books, and seminars for the novelties and grabbers, which will, we hope, enable us to hold on for another season.

Although the purpose of this book is to investigate concepts, a few illustrations might help us translate our philosophy into specific programs. What kinds of programs should be promoted? How can we achieve the full promise of this sacred endeavor? How do we get there from here?

IN THE BEGINNING

To get off to the best possible start, the local church must, from the beginning, (1) pledge itself to some basic youth-ministries commitments, (2) assume the costs of this effort, and

(3) perceive the benefits accruing to the church conscientiously engaged in this immense task.

The church that claims to be interested in meaningful youth work needs to see it as a *specialized ministry*. It is specialized because of the peculiarities of adolescent development and their unique environment. Youth ministry is a cross-cultural mission, requiring a special calling and special sensitivity. The fully integrated multigenerational church is ideal but generally not a reality until a separate and viable youth fellowship is well established.

The church must be committed to *consistent quality* in the leadership and programming of its youth ministry. Teenagers have more free time and are more available than any other age-group. At the same time, their restlessness, mistrust, and hard-to-please attitude is legendary. They are only attracted to activities that are set up with their needs and tastes in mind. They can only develop satisfying relationships with adults who are available on a fairly regular basis. Churches are well-advised to note the high standards indicated here, which are compromised only at the peril of losing the interest of those we want to reach.

The church has to recognize youth ministry as a *deliberate priority*. It does not happen accidentally, nor does it happen when it is consigned to a seldom-recognized niche in a larger list of concerns. Adolescence is the transitional moment of decision. If we miss them now, we may forfeit any influence—for the duration of their lives. There is an urgency about this special attention that may not be quite as intense in other areas of ministry. They are more vulnerable than children and more open to inducements than adults.

Before initiating a youth ministry, the church must count the cost and anticipate the benefits. The costs include personnel expenses, an adequate support budget, use of the church's facilities, the time and energies of volunteers, and the recognition of young people as a significant constituency within the church.

The "pay off" will be apparent. There will be the injection

of youthful enthusiasm and new spiritual life. It will allow outreach through kids to their families (very often the youth ministry can "pay" for itself as members are added to the body). It will provide a dynamic youth fellowship that offers guidance, teaching, counseling, positive peer reinforcement, and an exciting, accepting social situation for the young people of the church and their friends in the community.

Should the church hire a youth minister? There is no simple answer, but it is quite apparent that a single individual (or two or three, as a very tight-knit unit) should assume primary responsibility for the implementation of this ambition. Whether he or she is paid, this person needs to dedicate many hours each week to providing the leadership essential to this formidable task. Churches usually end up doing what they truly believe in, in spite of the obstacles or price tags. We crusade for pipe organs, repaved parking lots, towering steeples, new carpeting, and overseas missions—there is always a way if we feel strongly enough about it. Should we not invest at least a nominal sum in human resources who can play a critical role in the lives of our teenagers?

The entire church, and particularly its key leaders, are asked to ponder this decision. Without an informed and prayerful endorsement that is integrated into the central purpose of the church's existence, youth ministry is not on firm ground.

THE STRUCTURE OF YOUTH MINISTRY

The creation of a ministry to youth is a process that demands strategic thinking. It is not conjured up in an instant, nor does it happen automatically after a certain period of time has passed. It is a spiritual construction project.

Jesus Christ is the foundation, the cornerstone, the ground of our youth ministry in at least three specific ways. First, He is the definitive *model*. We should consciously emulate the precedents and principles of His supreme pattern.

Second, He is not only our historical example; He is our contemporary and, therefore, the *source* for all we seek to accomplish. Empowered by His Spirit, we need to submit ourselves daily to the Lord and rely on His strength to face with courage and grace the difficult, the frustrating, the distasteful, the demoralizing, and the impossible.

Third, His is the *glory*. It is ultimately His ministry done for His kids in His power. This liberates us from beguiling yet debilitating success fantasies. It is all through Him and for Him, and the most marvelous achievements should invoke accolades for Him. Those of us who are privileged to work for Christ are His grateful bond-slaves.

This project may be represented in the following way:

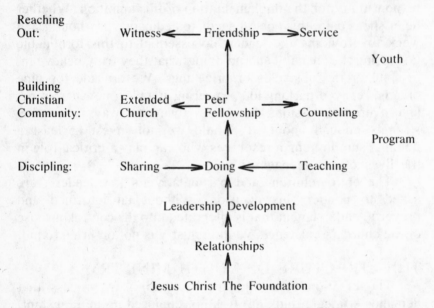

Reaching Out: Witness ← Friendship → Service

Youth

Building Christian Community: Extended Church ← Peer Fellowship → Counseling

Program

Discipling: Sharing → Doing ← Teaching

Leadership Development

Relationships

Jesus Christ The Foundation

We prepare for youth ministry by renewing our devotional experience with God. The spiritual disciplines must be in place in our own lives for us to answer the call positively and march into the fray. It is our deepest responsibility to make sure that the spiritual foundation for ourselves and for our ministry is intact.

Once we have reaffirmed our communion with God as His responsive children, we can move out aggressively and cultivate a broad range of relationships with teenagers, their parents, and other adults in the church, as well as with young people and adults in the community at large. All we are doing is making friends. We extend ourselves without a prepared agenda, without a compulsion to proselytize, and without the need to judge another's usefulness to us. We are getting acquainted, observing, listening, and inviting ourselves into positions where we may be of some use to others.

This openness takes time and ought to characterize our ministry throughout its tenure. This circle of relationships should be ever-widening even as we acknowledge our limitations. This keeps us fresh, in touch, credible, open to new opportunities for ministry, and visible as an illustration of what we exhort others to consider. Too many Christian leaders either start out looking for shortcuts to reaching the faceless masses with spectacular programs, or end up in relative seclusion, devoting themselves to elitist chores.

As we mingle in a greater variety of settings, we should keep an eye open for adults who might be prospective youth leaders. Youth ministry is not a solo performance. A small dose of wisdom will convince us of the surpassing value of team ministry. The youth minister (paid or not) will function as the leader of the leaders. He or she is a talent scout, always eager to recruit others whom God may be prompting to join in the cause.

Leadership development for youth ministry is a vast and complex topic. It deserves its own book. Its pivotal position in the structure of ministry, as that piece that directly supports the entire cluster of programs, clinches its importance. It is the team of leaders that carries out the ministry, not the omnigifted, edict-dispensing, quietly desperate, lonely figure of the youth minister. The one-man show is much less effective than the team.

Within a few months, the original leader should be in partnership with at least one other. One plus one, in the geometric progression of leadership effectiveness, equals three or more.

Youth work requires both male and female adult leaders. A mix of attributes and backgrounds has advantages. In summary, the team approach to ministry is mandated by these compelling considerations:

• More personalized contact with kids is possible.
• More work is accomplished.
• A wider range of abilities is represented.
• Leadership morale and support is generally better.
• A more objective view of the state of the ministry is gained.
• A high-profile model of Christian community is exhibited.
• Personal coverage for boys and girls is offered.
• The confidence of concerned observers (other adults) is increased.
• The leader of the leaders is able to spend part of his or her time in long-range planning.
• The almost mystical power of networking has a cumulative effect.
• Individual leaders are prone to stay longer, correct weaknesses, and grow faster when they are motivated by a team in pursuit of transcendent goals.
• It is easier to recruit a new leader into a team situation.

The traditional terminology used to identify leaders in youth ministry often reflects an inadequate concept of their roles. The *advisor* (shouting advice from a distance), the *chaperone* (along for the ride to keep order), the *sponsor* (a patronizing well-wisher conned into showing up once in a while), or *parents-on-rotation* (taking their turn at babysitting) all fall short of capturing the lofty call to youth ministry and of facilitating the kind of interpersonal friendship that is the touchstone of true ministry. Volunteer leaders should not simply assist the youth minister (the leader of the leaders) as a favor; they need to be sure that God is commissioning them and that the other members of the team are their colleagues, co-workers, fellow ministers. Anything less is a temporary provision—mercenary and usually inept.

The leader of the leaders should personally invite those who seem to have a lively walk with God, a heart for kids, an open mind, the interest, and some time to spend, to attend and observe the group for a period of three to six weeks. During that time, the prospective leader can watch at close range and interact with the kids and other leaders with no obligations. Also during that time, the visitor can look over the group, catch the ethos of the ministry, and decide whether this would be a good opportunity.

A follow-up conversation will discover whether to proceed. Complete honesty is essential at this stage. Do we (the leader and the prospective leader) like what we see? Are there any reservations on either side? Were we comfortable working with each other? Does there appear to be a basic compatibility? What are the chances that this person will become an assertive/submissive servant-leader of kids? We should earnestly pray for corroboration of our conclusions.

If the signs are positive, we can hammer out a tentative but fairly specific agreement. It can be customized to suit the person but must include a pledge to consistent, regular involvement; a wholehearted commitment to the team; plans to be further equipped for the task; start-up program assignments according to interests and gifts; and the understanding that personal contacts with kids outside the formal program are eventually to become part of the responsibility.

This sounds strenuous. It is. Qualified individuals need to be trained, encouraged, and shown how to do it. Keep in mind that a diminished challenge defeats the promise and ends up demeaning both the adults and young people involved. Less happens because we ask for less and dilute our high calling.

Obviously an individual cannot hold several offices in the church and do "a little youth work" on the side. That is a delusion and an insult to the kids. Much frustration and disillusionment is avoided when the full implications of this ministry are communicated in advance. We should perennially renew our vision so as not to slip into a complacent, cold, ingrown, bureaucratic mockery of authentic ministry. At present we seem to be wasting the time and talents of many who have not been sufficiently challenged or enabled to make their best attempt.

Youth leaders need constant nurturing. But they should receive their primary spiritual food outside the specific youth programs and should not expect their needs to be met by the kids.

The cohesion of the team ought to be one of the highest priorities. Without the integrity of that comradeship, the ministry emanating from it is compromised.

The leadership team needs to spend time together away from the maddening crowd. We are not seeking a businesslike relationship but an experience of "life together" out of which flows a torrent of ministry. This arduous project of building a team actually slows us down initially, but after a while its fruitfulness is evident. Bypassing this level to fabricate an instantly impressive and well-oiled machine is a shortcut that turns out to be a cul-de-sac. The siren song of overnight success in a youth ministry run exclusively by the hired hand should not be heeded.

When our team gets going, the process tends to move in this sequence: (1) personal sharing, apart from the details of the program; (2) preparation (the preview); (3) participation in activities (the experience); and (4) reflection (the debriefing).

The leader of the leaders manages this cycle so that the team is able to fulfill its charter expeditiously. This person must see that communication is current and accurate, and he or she must be capable of diagnosing breakdowns in the system as well as understanding the different attitudes and moods of the leaders. In addition, it is this person's responsibility to insure that the necessary resources are provided. Finally, the leader of the leaders occasionally directs discussions on the nature and purpose of the ministry to reformulate a consensus and make any requisite adjustments.

A subsequent priority at this level is to develop a student leadership team that is the identifiable core of the youth group. I believe that this should be accomplished by approaching a small number of the most mature young people in the group individually, rather than holding a popular election of officers. The latter practice, in my view, emphasizes mostly irrelevant qualities, setting up figureheads who arouse jealousy and who are not disposed to take their mandate to serve seriously after the polls are closed.

What we need is a working team—young people who are not in it for the prestige (there is no parade where these peer leaders flaunt their status) and who are responsive to us and capable of making things happen. Their opinions are given high regard, functioning as counterpoint to the sometimes parochial assumptions of the adults. Ideally, the adult and student leadership will work side-by-side, blending their efforts into a prodigious servant force.

Discipleship has emerged as a catchword for youth ministry in the past several years. At times it has taken on authoritarian overtones as if youth ministers were mass-producing junior clones. That is unfortunate and dangerous. Biblically sensitive zeal for discipleship exercises an influence that encourages young people to discover and fulfill the unique destiny God has appointed for them.

Like us, our fellow leaders, whether they are adults or adolescents, are disciples in training. An approximation to the image of the perfect humanity of Jesus Christ is what we seek for ourselves and for the kids we love. We must renounce any aspiration to lord it over anyone, declaring instead His Lordship and our final accountability to Him.

Nevertheless, our involvement with the other leaders can produce life-changing results. If we humbly deflect any credit, recognize that the authority we have is derived, and preserve their inviolable freedom, we may eagerly pursue the ends of discipleship.

This process creates followers of Jesus Christ; it does not manufacture or mass produce them. The Holy Spirit is working through us and in them to cultivate the spiritual fruit and underlying changes that He superintends. This is not an option only for the super-spiritual but a lifestyle to be entered into by all who claim to be Christians.

Discipleship is the ultimate adventure—not a perfectionistic performance of dreary religious duties. Christian discipleship can be transplanted to the youth culture; it is not just reserved for settled, middle-aged adults (a sixteen-year-old believer, growing in her faith, still has a right to be and act sixteen). Discipleship is a lifetime journey, and signs of its progress in teenagers are delightful.

In our overall program scheme, discipleship entails three components: teaching, sharing, and doing. Teaching is the educational, more intellectual, part. There is a time for adult leaders to provide input. Biblical exposition, topical presentations, and even the illumination of ponderous theological themes, as well as expressions direct from the heart of the youth leader, are all vital.

There also need to be regular times of interaction. Personal sharing at an emotional level is a healthy way of deciphering and integrating acquired information. Reactions to the facts, descriptions, and interpretations will surface. How do they feel about what they have heard? What are they struggling with? Where are they confused? How does all of this apply to them? An open discussion of relevant issues and questions in a safe, permissive setting is a missing component in many youth groups.

Finally, both the teaching and the sharing provoke young people to try to do what they sense Christ is asking them to do. Bible study alone is not the same as discipleship; nor is listening to an eloquent message evidence that discipleship is taking place. Talking about doing God's will is still only on the brink of discipleship. True disciples are more than learners, memorizers, patrons, and fervid devotees of God's Word—they are doers of the Word. They have taken a volitional leap.

Discipleship, whether it takes place one-on-one or in a small group, must press toward an answer to the urgent question: "So what are we going to do about it?" We become accountable to each other when we choose to grow. We comfort and exhort one another when we fail; we cheer each other on when Christlikeness is being attained. We are not afraid of problems or struggles or failures. We remind each other of Christ's presence and the hope that He guarantees.

I have seen young people thrive on this opportunity. We need to make it available for those who are ready. Adult leaders who are maturing in their own experience with the Lord and are deeply caring for individual kids act as catalysts for this process. The internalization and demonstration of the life of Christ is the objective, which is worth every effort and sacrifice.

Methods of discipleship abound. Although every leader must discover his or her own way, I will suggest the following sequence as a point of reference:

Phase 1: The adult leaders participate in a small discipleship group of their own peers.

Phase 2: A prototype discipleship group, guided by the leader of the leaders and including one or two other adults and at least three kids, is launched. The objective of the group is explained at the first session, and a short-term (perhaps six to eight weeks) timetable is set.

The format for this group and for the groups that follow the experimental model might be ordered in this fashion:

(a) Small talk upon arrival.

(b) An icebreaker question, getting everyone talking and introducing the Scripture passage or topic in a way that connects with the mundane interests of kids.

(c) A discussion sheet is handed out that outlines a series of main points and questions. Stick with one or two paragraphs of a passage—probe for practical implications. (Matthew 3–7; James; Philippians; excerpts from Proverbs; 1 John; a Minor Prophet; Romans 12; Hebrews 11, 12; 1 Corinthians 12, 13; Ephesians; and Revelation 1–3 are only a sampling of the slices of the Word that can be digested and enrich our lives.)

(d) Prayer for each other.

(e) Go out together or play together afterward.

Phase 3: Each experienced, trained leader takes four to eight kids and forms a new group (we expect other kids to become interested). Dividing by boys and girls, by geographic area, or by special interest are all plausible tactics. The leaders may want to work through the same book on parallel tracks. Group leaders should try to be alone with each individual in the group once a month. Once in a while, all the groups can come together or, perhaps, go away together to reinforce their common objective.

Phase 4: The peer discipleship group can stimulate tremendous growth. But some qualified adults and interested kids are not available at the scheduled times or require special attention. Coupling youth leaders and other kindly adults in the church with young people can be very profitable (the leader of the leaders will need to consult with these free-lance ministers). Older, mature youth can work with their younger peers. New Christians, especially, need faithful care. Some who are more advanced can benefit from an accelerated program.

Most church youth ministries carry on a program that could be labeled "fellowship." A little bit of Bible study, a little bit of fun, a little bit of evangelism—a little bit of almost anything simmered into a lowest-common-denominator broth of ministry. It is a diluted compromise of various objectives that attempts to ration out the minimum weekly requirements to the kids of the church to keep them coming and reasonably happy. But it is too often a thin, insipid gruel that keeps us going—barely.

What we wish for is a dynamic peer fellowship where we celebrate the gifts of God's grace and of each other. Such an atmosphere is characterized by openness, depth, joy, and appreciation for our diversity as well as our solidarity. Problems can be solved, wounds healed, temptations resisted, and spiritual desires ignited.

Is this a realizable dream or a fantasy for a group of average college, senior-high, or junior-high people? If the New Testament is not simply tantalizing us, I think we can expect to at least get a taste of this supernatural experience of divine-human community (God is here among us, is He not?).

Very often the new youth minister inherits a shell of a youth fellowship program. It is not satisfactory for anyone, yet it cannot be quickly scuttled either. There are many advantages to starting from scratch with the luxury of spending several months concentrating on the devotional, relational, and leadership development priorities. But this is not generally possible, and radical disruptions prematurely imposed are not advised.

We can begin without making any structural changes in the existing program because early on we are preoccupied with getting to know the kids and introducing ourselves. Eventually we will want to make adjustments, though we understand that alterations in the program do not, in and of themselves, determine success or failure. As the leadership team develops and individuals are discipled, the beneficial effects of high-quality relationships within the group will be felt. The activities become meaningful and attractive as we enjoy being with each other. The activities by themselves cannot carry the load. Young Christians who are discovering their special place in God's heart and in His family will have a good time doing almost anything together. This slightly hyperbolic statement instructs us to put more effort into developing the right kind of environment than we do into devising an enthralling calendar of events.

Ordinarily, young people need to feel secure within their peer fellowship and to experience a degree of satisfaction there before they are willing to integrate themselves into the larger church body. We might lament this fact, but we must take it seriously. Since younger children usually attend separate Sunday-school classes, the worship service appears to the adolescent to be an assembly of older adults. Very few teenagers are prepared to commit themselves to a congregation unless they come in a group of friends their own age.

Eventually, the youth leaders must find ways to facilitate this commitment to a larger fellowship because a lifelong participation in the Body of Christ is at stake. On the other hand, youth leaders are obliged not only to educate the kids and gently encourage them in this direction but also to advocate for their needs and interests before the other pastors and elders. Adaptation is a two-way street, and there is much to be gained by everyone.

The *extended church* refers to other local, regional, national, and international expressions of the church of Jesus Christ, as well as the full membership of our own particular fellowship. Our kids can benefit immensely from contact with other groups. It is encouraging to note how broad and varied and fascinating this Christian movement is. It is a marvelous conspiracy. To interact with our brothers and sisters, who are different from and yet like us, sharpens our insights.

Within our peer fellowship we will encounter individuals whose problems necessitate attention outside the group setting. It may be a sudden crisis or a chronic difficulty that occasions the opportunity for counseling. This is a significant part of our ministry.

It is not the same as discipling, which has long-term spiritual development as its focus. Counseling is usually a short-term undertaking that seeks to address and ameliorate a pressing need. If the difficulty requires a professional to be brought in for counseling sessions, then we must make use of such auxiliary help without losing track of the person.

Many, if not most, church youth ministries never get around to doing outreach ministry with any consistency or seriousness. It is, admittedly, a forbidding assignment, but we must get to it. The church does not exist just to serve us and take care of "our kids." We are called, eventually, to build bridges into our community.

I do not believe that an outreach campaign can happen right away. The young people in our fellowship first need to feel comfortable with each other and enjoy being together before they will invite or appreciate newcomers. The fellowship, in turn, will not become this kind of place until at least a few core kids are on a discipleship course. And again, until we have a coterie of committed Christlike adult leaders who are sharing their lives with these kids, we are prevented from flourishing at any of the program levels.

Thus, our ability to reach those outside the church is dependent on a sturdy scaffolding of ministry and upon the solicitous welcome offered by those who are already part of the fellowship. It is obviously important for the adult leaders to befriend all visitors to the youth program, and it is even more critical for strangers to sense the acceptance of their peers. Their peers are the glue that help the tentative first-timer stick. It is humbling for the leadership to realize that it is generally not the powerful speaking, wonderful music, spectacular media presentations, outstanding facility, schedule of exciting activities, or even well-organized-for-fun games (all of which are terrific advantages) that keep the passers-by with us and poised to meet the Lord. Initially, they may be attracted by these program features. But all of that is simply a means of bringing us together. Once we are together, the quality of the relationships will distinguish the group. The new people and the regular members will only come if they trust the other people there and feel accepted. Of course, there may be some who come because they were ordered to, but the leadership should not be content if that is the only reason.

At first, outreach is a matter of simply extending ourselves in friendship to another person. It can be done spontaneously on neutral turf or by design in a program setting geared to those who do not yet know God. To get to know that person and to be known are our desires. But ultimately, friendship is not enough, though it is a natural beginning. We look forward to that opportunity to witness the remedy, the fulfillment, the answer that this person might not yet even realize he or she needs. In our relationships and in our programs, we lovingly wait and then lovingly express our faith.

If our friendship is sincere, we must be available for practical service. We must back our sentiments and words with actions on behalf of those we declare we care for. Youth ministry should provide opportunities for work experiences that benefit others. Evangelism-by-word and service-by-deed fulfill the direct command to reach out to a lost and hurting world. If we fail to bring our kids to this level of understanding and personal commitment, we jeopardize the mission of the church and settle for a civic social club or a secret saints society.

It has been my experience that once ministry is properly established—when relationships are strong and individuals are growing—we are primed for the priority of outreach. Even though it is not quite effortless, it is an extremely uplifting new chapter in the ongoing saga of ministry.

During my first year as a full-time youth worker, contacting and hanging on to new folks seemed impossible. I confess that I moved too fast at times and alienated some who were not yet confident of my love. But once we were ready, there was virtually no way to turn off the steady stream of kids dropping in on us, and they did not come to hear me or anyone else deliver a show-stopping message. When God begins to add to our numbers and bolster our spiritual vitality, youth ministry is the most exciting earthly experience imaginable.

What happens after outreach has been accomplished? Actually, we never stop doing it. It remains the cutting edge of our ministry. There is always another person, another clique, more "unreachables," the hidden and unknown peoples in our own community, those on the fringe, new territories, and the world beyond.

We will never be done. We must always be shoring up the foundations of our ministry and reminding ourselves of our first love. As we strive to build a comprehensive ministry, we will discover problems and challenges that we overlooked before. Then, as momentum increases, we can take some time out to advise others who are just starting. However, our joy as well as our credibility remain in being actively involved on the front lines. The battlefield, it seems, is beleaguered by war-weariness and stretches out forever, but the victories Christ achieves through (and despite) us—His co-combatants in the trenches— more than compensate for the trouble.

INTIMATIONS OF THE STRUCTURE

This view of ministry development resolves several distressing questions and dilemmas that often arise:

Should we go with quantity or quality in our outreach and discipleship? The answer is both. This structure helps us to interpret the sequence and the relationship of the two. Discipleship becomes the basis for expansion, and the challenges of reaching out stimulate growth in discipleship. To invest in both is mutually enhancing. Intensification (in-depth spiritual growth) and extension (the attempt to grow numerically) are our two nonnegotiable goals.

Should we be more concerned with evangelism or social action? This is another false polarity. It dissolves as we acknowledge the necessity of both activities. We do not have the luxury of choosing between them.

Are intellectual concepts, emotional engagement, or active obedience to God's Word what we wish to emphasize? Again, all are important.

Is youth ministry segregated from the rest of the church? Yes and no. A grasp of the particular dynamics informs us of how we ought to proceed in each case.

Is youth ministry concerned with programs or people? The answer is both, if we are aware that programs are crafted to serve the needs of kids. A program is a plan, a format, an organization, and a deployment of resources that will help us reach people. On one hand, pure programming is nonsense; on the other, desiring to minister to people without a premeditated approach is irresponsible.

We build from the ground up. The cornerstone has already been laid. We derive our ministry from His. Eventually we want to establish programs that are channels of ministry, meeting needs at every level. The leader of the leaders and the adult leadership team are deliberately at the bottom of the three levels of programmed ministry: Christ serves us; we serve the kids; the more mature Christian young people serve others who have pressing needs. As kids become more interested, they move toward and into the discipling mode and then, possibly, into leadership positions. Accordingly, we can expect a healthy structure to include greater numbers at the higher levels.

If there is a weakness at any level, we "building inspectors" should search for the cause in the level beneath it. Each program's effectiveness is limited by the group supporting it. If we can create a strong leadership team, get started with discipleship, and prepare to take some radical risks in reaching out, we are well on our way to fulfilling the dream.

THE "COSMOLOGY" OF DISCIPLESHIP

It is our deepest desire, in youth ministry, to encourage each young person to take the next step toward a more mature relationship with Jesus Christ. We do not prejudge where people ought to be; we are simply glad to take them the next step from where they are. We must determine where each person is on their pilgrimage and confirm that our ministry works to facilitate their next steps. The following illustration can assist us in evaluating our program and the young people in it.

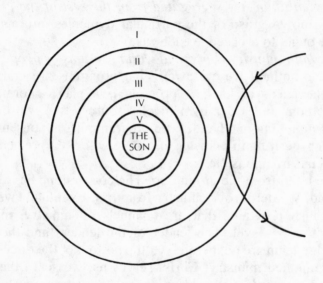

This analogy is borrowed from our solar system. Jesus Christ Himself is the sun. Those who are outside of the influence of the Son—of His gravitational pull—are wandering on their own courses, unenlightened by the source of all illumination. The five concentric circles represent orbits of varying proximity to the sun:

1. *Friendship.* A person's first positive contact with Christianity is often through acquaintance with a believer. This friendship retrieves them from the empty, dark, and chaotic

domain outside of Christ and locks them (at least temporarily) into a peripheral orbit, bringing them into the warmth and attraction of the Son. This is an ideal introduction because it is personal and not threatening.

2. *Exposure*. Gradually, with sensitive consideration for the needs, desires, and background of the individual, he or she needs to hear the Good News. The message should be winsome, relevant, clear, and true to its source. The Christian friend needs to point beyond himself, witnessing to the center of his faith.

3. *Decision*. Eventually this person needs to be confronted with the challenge to commit his or her life to Christ. Within the context of friendship and an intelligent understanding of the gospel, this person now needs to be encouraged to make the decision to move into a personal relationship with Christ. Until this commitment is made, the person is always in danger of behaving like a comet—appearing for a while to be with us, but then shooting off into outer space.

4. *Implantation*. A conversion experience must be followed by active participation in the Christian community. This person is now part of a galaxy of believers who comprise the Body of Christ. The person becomes a star in the constellation and is nurtured by this celestial association. Faith and knowledge grow as this person takes full advantage of the resources of God's people.

5. *Ministry*. It is God's will for us to translate our faith and nourishment into ministry. We reflect the Son most brilliantly when we give ourselves away in loving service and become an effective means of drawing others closer to the One who is "brightest and best."

PROGRAMMING CONSIDERATIONS
THE WEEKLY SCHEDULE

We must think carefully about the arrangement of our regularly scheduled activities. We should be able to place each program in the larger structure of ministry, remembering that the principle objective of each activity should be clear to the leadership. As our ministry develops, we should be able to specify our goals for every program. We have to provide for the appropriate needs at all three levels while producing a reasonable, workable schedule.

A great variety of problems can arise as we try to implement a weekly program schedule:

Sunday burnout: A burdensome line-up of back-to-back programs concentrated on Sunday (Sunday school followed by morning service, youth choir, youth leadership, evening service, youth fellowship, and so on). This schedule not only leaves everyone (leaders and youth alike) exhausted, but it also gives the impression that Sunday is for religion, and the rest of the week we are on our own. A double standard is implied. Furthermore, Sunday outreach programs may be unrealistic— many young people may feel that to attend they must have the same church affiliation.

Irregular scheduling. This leaves everyone guessing where and when the next program is.

Programs that compete with family, school, or other social activities. Sometimes this will happen, but we need to calculate the values and costs involved in constantly competing with other activities.

Too many nights out. We do not want to wear the kids out, strain their parents' good will, or have so many programs that we cannot adequately prepare for them. There is no virtue in a heaping quantity of mediocrity.

One all-purpose program per week. If the above regimen threatens to run us ragged, this light fare severely limits our options in responding to a variety of needs. We ought to anticipate the scheduling opportunities and plan accordingly. We should ensure an optimal setting each week for teaching, sharing, and discipleship; reaffirming fellowship; and providing an effective outreach program.

One way to accomplish this is to consolidate programs on two days of the week: Sunday (avoiding too many activities that require sitting still) and a late afternoon or weeknight, which leaves weekends available for occasional special events. This makes it easier on the parents (we only commandeer their children for one evening during the week), on the kids, and on ourselves. When we come together, there is a reason, an expectation of a meaningful experience, and a realization that other demands on our agenda are being respected. A full—though not overwhelming—and attractive schedule of Christian education classes, athletics, youth choir, discipleship groups, outreach meetings, and leadership briefings, as well as major worship services, can be comfortably fit into the week. The leadership brigade should meet together about once a month for extended and practical discussion.

Shutting a program down for the summer, as happens in many places, is a questionable tradition. Kids have more free time in the summer: they have no homework; they can stay out later; the warm weather is better for outdoor activities; and summer is "up" time for teenagers. Although many of them work and take family vacations, there will still be many young people just hanging around during any given week, and most kids are available if there is something worthwhile going on.

THE MAIN EVENT

Most youth groups are known for the program that draws the largest number of people each week. In a very real sense, this event becomes our public image; it establishes our reputation. It is probably the place where most kids first make contact with the group.

This program, most likely, is concerned either with outreach or fellowship. There are many ways to set up this experience, but the following, rather generic flow chart shows the principal elements.

There is a moment of transition between phases, which, we hope, sets up the mood and goals of the next phase. As the program progresses, we generally look for a greater group cohesion, a calming down, and a focus of interest. The following commentary outlines what we expect during the one-to-two-hour period:

Transition: If we cannot get the kids there, nothing else matters. We want to work on good publicity, a positive reputation, a program plan that we believe will be of interest to them, as well as select the most convenient day and time.

Transition 1   Phase

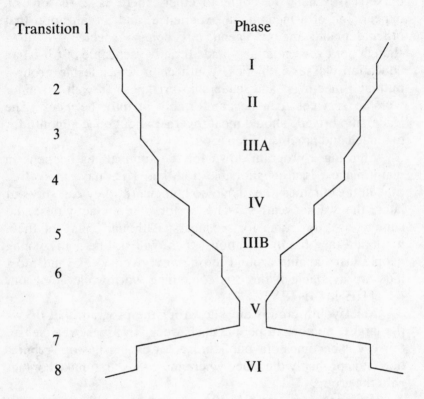

Phase I: *Prelude.* Before the program officially starts, we want to mix with the early arrivals, meet new people, and by our presence create a warm and welcoming atmosphere.

Transition: A few minutes after the scheduled starting time, we want to bring everyone together (in one group or in subgroups).

Phase II: *Games.* We hope to arouse their excitement and lower inhibitions by involving everyone in the organized fun (indoors or outdoors).

Transition: We may need to physically rearrange the room

and get people a little less rowdy, and probably seated, at this juncture.

Phase IIIa: *Lively Singing.* We can take advantage of music (recorded, performed, conducted by a song leader) as a spirited and unifying medium.

Transition: At this point we need a change of pace, getting everyone's attention for the next segment, perhaps by building some suspense.

Phase IV: *Warm-up and Transition—Skits and Announcements.* This gives us a break to clown around a bit, report news to the group, and promote future activities, as well as a chance to make use of several people up front. By the end of this interlude we need to "have them."

Phase IIIb: *Inspirational Singing.* This introduces a more mellow mood, perhaps immediately before the message.

Transition: By this time the group should almost be ready for the spiritual content of the evening; they may need a brief and respectful yet serious request for their complete attention for the next few moments.

Phase V: *Message—Talk, Personal Witness, Drama, Film, Special Music, Group Discussion, Prayer.* This should provide an interesting, relevant, personal, and compelling presentation of some aspect of the faith.

Transition: A thoughtful pause can serve to assimilate the impact of what has preceded.

Phase VI: *Postlude.* We need to set aside some time afterward to mingle, make appointments, invite and sign up kids for special events, and, possibly, serve refreshments.

Transition: We trust that everyone departs with a favorable impression of the experience, looks forward to upcoming activities, considers the personal implications of this program, and is anxious to tell others what has happened.

PROGRAM CYCLE

Every program goes through a cycle of development. We need to perceive the logic of this sequence and help it along. The progression looks something like this:

169

personal preparation ◊ background research ◊ program creation ◊ program establishment ◊ growth ◊ consolidation ◊ innovation ◊ growth

At the beginning, the leader must be certain to review his or her vision and qualifications for this venture. Next, the leader must do some homework, discerning needs, checking resources, examining various problems, and consulting with those whose opinions may be significant.

Then, if everything looks positive, the program is launched. After it is under way, its value must be demonstrated and momentum must gather. As word gets around and more kids join the program, a period of growth should be expected.

At some later point it will become necessary to reevaluate the effectiveness of the program in light of its original goals. We need to be sure we are on still on the track. This review will cause us to contemplate innovations, and not simply to sustain what has become a tradition. Adjustments are occasionally necessary.

Finally, we may have a new growth spurt. This repeating cycle of growth, consolidation, innovation, and more growth may continue for a long while. But there may be times when we should consider putting an obsolete or impractical program out of its misery and beginning the process over again with a new set of plans.

A PROGRAM SAMPLER OF SPECIAL EVENTS

Briefly, I will list a few of the many possibilities for special scheduled activities. If the regular weekly program is a nourishing and flavorful entrée, then these special activities are the sparkling appetizers and sumptuous desserts. Space allows only a brief list, but there is a veritable mountain of resources that can fill in the details and provide other ideas.

- *Retreats:* overnight or for a weekend—with just one group or with others—at a local or distant facility.
- *Wilderness adventures:* backpacking, canoeing, rafting, bicycling, camping, day hiking, mountain climbing.
- *Mission work projects:* local, cross-cultural.

- *Parties:* seasonal, theme.
- *Banquets.*
- *Concerts.*
- *Day trips:* beaches, amusement parks, sporting events.
- *Picnics.*
- *Recreation:* volleyball, softball, roller-skating, ice-skating, bowling, swimming, water-skiing, snow-skiing, basketball, football, new games, square dancing, folk games.
- *Fund raising.*
- *Summer camps.*
- *Special conferences.*
- *Topical seminars.*
- *Tours:* choir/ensemble, to another church or city.

All activities should be done with the goals of ministry in mind. As youth leaders, we are not to occupy kids' time just to give them something to do. In all we do, we seek to convey God's love and concern to those we are with. The quality of our time together should reflect this conscious commitment, as we accept teenagers wherever they are and for whatever reasons they have come. It is our responsibility to serve and care for them as people while we orchestrate an appealing and potentially influential program.

UTILIZING RESOURCES

It is a mistake to reproduce someone else's program, no matter how successful it has been. Every church has unique priorities and different needs that should be taken into account. However, it is not inappropriate to copy certain aspects of another program that might succeed in your particular circumstance. By all means, let us beg, borrow, and steal ideas from each other, but let us also thoughtfully improvise. We will become the experts on what works best and why.

We need access to resources, and fortunately, the repertoire for programming is expanding rapidly. As we peruse the literature and question our colleagues, we must analyze and adapt material for our setting and purposes. We should range widely in our search with a voracious curiosity for, as well as a certain skepticism about, new ideas and formulas.

There are many questions we should ask as we consider a possible program:

- What goal is reached by making use of it?
- Does it fit into our program and ministry objectives?
- Do I understand it? Can I visualize it?
- Do I like it?
- Would the kids like it?
- Can I trust the originator of this resource?
- How much time, effort, and cost is required to do it?
- Do we have the right talent to lead it?
- Do we have the right number of people for it?
- What kind of setup is required?
- Do I have time to orient the other leaders to it?
- What risks are involved in doing it?
- If it fails, how bad will it be?
- If it works, how valuable could it be?
- What experiences have others had with it?

The following suggestions may help in the creative and effective use of resources in programming:

- Sample widely; get on mailing lists. Talk to other leaders frequently. Become a walking index of ideas.
- Mix the tried-and-true with the novel. Cover the risk. Keep it fresh, but do not try to be radically different all the time.
- Preview the resource first if possible (especially if there is a major commitment of emphasis, time, or money).
- Take advantage of free offers.
- Remember that the youth leaders control the use of the idea and can modify it to suit their group's needs.
- Find the gold mines—those sources that consistently bring out quality ideas and products.
- Develop personal relationships with key resource people

and organizations. Ask for tips from those informants who are in-the-know.

- If there is any doubt about the integrity of a resource or its sponsor, investigate thoroughly before using.
- The first time a new idea is used, keep a very close watch on it.
- When a familiarity with the conventional resources has been attained, experiment with variations and invent entirely new forms.

The felicitous application of program resources and ideas depends on the leader's level of awareness, experience, instinct for how kids respond, self-confidence, credibility rating with the kids, recognition and acceptance by other adults who have clout, good judgment, flexibility, and understanding of the nature of ministry. It is heartening to note that both knowledge of and skill with the resources and elements of programming are cumulative for the individual and compounded in the aggregate of the leadership team.

DELEGATION

There is no way any one of us could or should try to do all of this alone. Without astute delegation of responsibilities, we will wallow in our own helpless inefficiency. "Divide and conquer" is our motto. The person who tries to do it all is a fool. (I say this as a periodic fool, myself, and with sympathy).

Every program can be broken down into its component parts and managed by a team working together. Once a fluid and practicable system is devised for each program, we find ourselves wasting less time and feeling less anxiety. It is worth spending a few hours designing the system so that we are free to give ourselves to the personal side of youth ministry.

We can begin to put together regular assignments for the weekly programs, mixing it up now and then to prevent predictability and rigid specialization. An ad hoc leadership committee, chaired by a trusted adult and student leaders with other kids invited to help out, is convened to plan, execute, and review each special activity. Not only will more leaders be involved in the effort and learning as a result, but there is a greater likelihood of better overall participation as more people respond to the highly motivated leaders.

As we appropriate this model and philosophy, our capacity for carrying out a dynamic, multifaceted ministry can be enlarged. The necessity of careful delegation of the demanding yet meaningful ministry chores is inevitably vindicated.

QUESTIONS

1. What has to happen for a church to begin a solid youth ministry? Has your church met these conditions?

2. With reference to the structure of youth ministry, how well built is your youth ministry? Have you constructed from the ground up? What level is now a priority for you?

3. Do you believe in team ministry? Are you a part of one?

4. Why is the terminology we use to describe youth leaders important? What significance is there in the designations you commonly use?

5. Have volunteer leaders been properly recruited, trained, and supported in your youth ministry? What needs to be done?

6. How can we evaluate the discipleship process? Is the urgent question, "So what are we going to do about it?" the punch line at your Bible study and sharing group?

7. How can we develop depth, purpose, and excitement in our small discipleship groups?

8. Why is our fellowship often superficial? What can we do about it?

9. Why do many church youth groups never implement serious, consistent outreach? How can leaders encourage it?

10. What is the relationship between outreach and fellowship? Between fellowship and discipleship? Between the youth program and leadership development?

11. What false polarizations are resolved by this proposed structure of ministry?

12. To what two uses can we put the "cosmology" of discipleship graphic? Can you find your kids? Can you help them?

13. Why is it very important to wisely design the weekly schedule? How does yours match up?

14. What elements of your "Big Meeting" are effective? What is missing? What can you do?

15. Can you fit your programs into the program cycle? Are you managing their progress?

16. Can you describe the potential ministry value of the different kinds of special events enumerated? What additional experience and knowledge would you like to have?

17. How does a youth leader become proficient in using program resources? What can you do to increase your awareness and capabilities?

8 CONFLICTS: RESOLUTION AND BEYOND

CRISIS IN MINISTRY

There is a nearly infinite variety of ways for youth leaders to get themselves into trouble. Sometimes we bring it upon ourselves by our own irresponsible actions. At other times, however, conflict is unavoidable—perhaps even an indication that our ministry is making progress. A youth ministry that seems to be sailing along, free of tension and disagreement, is probably only standing still.

Youth ministry tends to breed a fighting spirit in its practitioners, and that, of course, is dangerous. A brooding belligerence is certainly not an asset. But the youth leader who always backs away from the sparks of confrontation has shamefully retreated from reality. Campaigning for self-advancement is an inglorious cause, but interposing oneself as a modest yet irrepressible champion of those in need is a worthy undertaking. Youth ministry, by nature, frequently defies the status quo. Things are not as they should be, and even if current conditions appear satisfactory, they can always be upgraded. For Christ's sake—and the kids'—we must press on toward solutions, growth, and excellence.

We need to remember that our fight is not against adversaries of flesh and blood. It is a more subtle, spiritual warfare, and we need all the allies we can get. As youth leaders, we are not out to make enemies—we want to be at peace with everyone— but we must realistically expect opposition. We will be misunderstood, blamed for the problems of the youth, doubted, criticized, and questioned at length about some of our "deviant'' practices. Expect someone to ask, "What do you do with all your free time, anyway, when you're not playing with the kids?'' We may, on some dark occasion, be forced to put our job security on the line. We must not retaliate with the weapons of conventional warfare: bitter sarcasm, mudslinging, name-calling, the silent treatment, fits of rage, personal attacks and unfair counteraccusations, spiteful sanctions, humiliating taunts, and divisiveness. Our means should be consistent with our ends. We brandish love, persuasion, competence, wisdom, forgiveness, perseverance, sacrifice, and humility. At least, this is our aim.

We must choose our battles carefully. A sense of proportion and timing is critical; the youth leader must make a rigorous distinction between preferences and convictions. To be at full strength for major confrontations, that is, bolstered by a record of gracious concessions and reasonable advocacies, is advantageous.

Several years ago as youth minister in a local church, I was preparing for a Sunday-evening teaching series for an intergenerational audience. The pastor (my boss) happened to stop by my office the week before the first session and suggested that it would be nice if I wore a suit and tie for this special assignment. This remark rankled me for two reasons: I was insulted that such a matter was not left to my professional discretion; and furthermore, on philosophical grounds, I felt that the most appropriate attire should approximate that of the other men in attendance, who dressed in a casual, open-collar style. So I sat there, feeling personally slighted and ideologically crossed.

What should I do? Should I go head-to-head with the pastor, call his bluff by reaffirming my position, and risk precipitating a battle-to-the-death over this hill of contention? I did, in fact, share my feelings with the pastor in a relatively calm voice. He listened politely but insisted I dress up anyway. He proceeded to pull rank (which he seldom did with me) to make it stick. The dilemma pitted my pride against an opportunity to comply and thereby gain leverage in other more strategic conquests later.

My pride lost that time—it should never be a weighty factor anyway. My ministry was not seriously hampered by my stunning three-piece suit, and the pastor later relented by permitting me to dress in torn jeans, a ripped shirt, and old tennis shoes, which I chose to wear one night to jolt the congregation into sensing their spiritual poverty as we studied the first Beatitude. Actually, this pastor was not averse to taking breathtaking risks in ministry. Iron banging iron sometimes yields surprisingly winning results.

Crises in youth ministry are inevitable. As we grow in our capacity to manage them, we begin to notice that such situations are ripe with potential for dramatic breakthroughs. A pastor with youth-ministry experience provides this interpretation:

> Fracturing crises are not abnormal in youth ministry. . . . The crisis does not mean that the group is bad, nor does it mean that the youth minister has failed. Sooner or later a crisis comes to everyone, and the youth minister does not need to feel that he or she is unqualified to lead young people.
>
> In fact, the resistance, the hours of discussion, and the debate about "The Problem" can actually be a strategy for self-organization by the youth group. On a deep level the group is growing up and learning how to deal realistically with its problems. Unless it can learn to work together and resolve conflict, it will never develop an effective ministry. What play does for children, conflict seems to do for teens.
>
> The long-term fruit of weathering a fracturing crisis is not a near defeat but something to build on. The youth group has proven that it will now be able to accommodate itself to unusual stresses it might face on the way to some of its ultimate goals.[1]

DISCIPLINE

I am convinced that problems requiring a disciplinary response to teenagers can ordinarily be held to an acceptable minimum. The burden is on us, as leaders, to create such a positively charged setting that there is little incentive to subvert it or concoct a counterprogram.

A boring program invites misbehavior. A relevant, upbeat

format tends to suppress wanton disruption. Leaders need to be hip to what is going on and not come off as oblivious substitute-teacher types. We must demonstrate personal interest. Beyond this, the whole mechanism of disciplinary ordinances should not be emphasized. Overcontrol is a fault of many youth programs, and it serves to aggravate, rather than repress, adolescent instincts to countermand authority. Heavy-handed policing is always offensive.

We must remind ourselves to plan and to lead with an awareness of the normal characteristics of adolescents. They need to express energy. They are groping toward independence. They are asking some very tough questions. To outlaw these habits is a losing policy. Not only must they be tolerated, but we are obliged to facilitate their constructive outlet.

It is essential that we attempt to diagnose the needs that underlie the problems that do flare up because often there is a deeper disturbance that is incidentally triggered by a proximate, secondary incident. If the youth leader shows respect for young people, the errant behavior is seldom a premeditated strike against him or her. We must learn patience and, very often, put up with immaturity while we work to strengthen an adolescent's self-image and build stability into the relationship.

Rebelliousness is preferable to passivity. Rebels are prime candidates for Christian service and leadership when their restlessness is redirected and harnessed for a higher purpose. I worry about those "good kids" who keep their thoughts to themselves. That is not a healthy way to live. Providing a safe place to vent forbidden thoughts and feelings (anger, uncertainties, envy, inadequacy) may be a cathartic experience. The rules have to be bent to accommodate individual needs.

Outright defiance, exhibiting a conscious and persistent disregard of the group, should be met with a controlled strength that spells out the options in the clearest terms. A firm response to repeated misdeeds is called for. But even when dealing with a hardened delinquent, we should extend our friendship—unconditionally and not as a bargaining chip. And we ought always to leave the door open for full restoration without lapsing into sponginess.

A youth leader cannot effectively discipline someone he does not know. Again, a sufficient number of caring leaders who initiate relationships can prevent many problems before they erupt. Often we can anticipate trouble and head it off by inserting ourselves into the nexus of the breakdown. The leader who is afraid of trouble, or who tries to crush it to prove his or her power, is courting disaster.

When correction becomes necessary, we need to proceed with caution. A lot is at stake. We are walking into the eye of the hurricane, and it is our earnest prayer that we all weather the storm and, together, make it through to the sunnier side. Instead of making suggestions, I offer the following, rather inflexible rules:

- First, determine that the individual or the group is being injured by the episode; be sure that it is not simply a problem or irritation for you.
- Make it a private matter. Never (except in a desperate emergency) rebuke a teenager in front of others.
- Practice confidentiality.
- Do not presume to understand another person's motives; share your observations of his or her behavior (it is useless to complain about attitude—that is too speculative and vague) and ask the individual, in an even, nonaccusatory tone, to explain the incident (for instance, "You seemed to be bored [or uncomfortable or angry] tonight—what's going on?").
- In a literal or figurative manner put your arm around the person creating the difficulty; be certain that a reprimand is not taken as rejection.
- Check back in a few days with the person you have challenged. When the initial sting from your verbal slap has subsided (no matter how nicely you say it, the person will recoil to some extent and feel badly), do not allow a distance to grow between you.

- Be respectful and reasonable, and listen to the other side of the story. If you were in error, admit it; but gently demand honesty.
- Compensate for the disciplinary affair with sincere, positive attention. Problem youths usually only hear from adults when something goes wrong.

Youth leaders are not watchdogs, drill sergeants, or undercover cops, but neither can they turn away from trouble. We should not allow ourselves to be intimidated, but we do not need to scare kids into submission. We seek to uphold our considerable responsibility *to* young people without assuming responsibility *for* their attitudes and behavior (though we should guarantee their physical safety while they are with us). Although we are not their parents, we should go to any extreme to help them. Although we are not their peers, we are at least as interested in them as any of their friends.

DISCORD

Only those who see themselves as full-fledged adults can minister to youth effectively. One of the problems that plagues younger youth leaders is not a lack of rapport with the kids, but an inability to relate directly and positively with older adults. A pastor recently wrote to me:

> It seems to me that one of the basic problems is the inability of the young leader to get along or work in an open way with adults in the church or, particularly, church officers. I'm sure you've tried to steer the students away from this and so it is perhaps a part of their growing experience . . . but how much frustration and unnecessary problems would be avoided if only the youth would not act as if they cannot talk to anyone over the age of thirty. The youth minister seems to side with the young people, often acts like them, and looks at the parents and adults like the enemy!
>
> Our situation is not unique. We've had three fine Christian young people who are talented and dedicated but who have caused so much trouble with the officers and leaders that I spend most of my time making sure there is some communi-

cation. They just stonewall every effort to evaluate them; they seldom talk to adults who are older than they are; they relate quite well with young people but appear aloof if not hostile toward older persons.

In addition to an involvement with young people, the youth minister is enmeshed in a vital network of liaisons with other adults. Who are these people, and how should we relate to them? There are several relationships that, because of their link to our ministry, could bear thoughtful examination.

The pastor/associate pastor/Christian-education director. The line of responsibility and reporting should be explicitly articulated. Within this arrangement, a collegial and informal atmosphere offers the best working conditions and evokes a reciprocal loyalty. The youth minister needs to have frequent contact with the supervisor. Checking in with new ideas is advisable and provides a cushion against sniping criticism about any departure from traditional expectations. At the same time, the nerve to go a few friendly but spirited rounds with one's political superior is not unseemly. Over time, the youth minister will discover that a well-informed, available, and supportive pastor is a precious gift.

Support staff. The secretarial and custodial personnel can be valuable aids (or barriers) to youth ministry. We must take them seriously and endeavor to win their regard by taking an interest in them and their work. General expectations should be hammered out so that a viable framework for problem solving exists when we suddenly need it. We should give advance notification of our requirements, demonstrating a sensitivity to their work load. Support staff should not dictate program policy, but youth ministry should not run roughshod over their legitimate concerns.

Boards and committees. My judgment is that a board or a committee should not exercise a supervisory function over the youth minister. Too many chiefs issuing directives is confusing and demoralizing. A board, acting in a supportive, advisory capacity and informed about the plans and results of the church's youth work, can run interference for us. Obviously, they have the right to raise questions about policy (if they have some input into our hiring, there should be no surprises here) and share personal concerns—actually, everybody has that privilege. But their authority to direct the day-to-day operation of youth ministry should be circumscribed. If there is a falling out, the pastor must intervene.

Parents. Alienating parents is suicidal in youth ministry. After all, youth work eventually leads to involvement with the family. Locating a cadre of parents committed to backing the youth program puts us miles ahead because they can help interpret our goals and find ways to reach other parents. Consistent communication with all the parents is mandatory—they want to be informed. This can be done through newsletters and occasional meetings. In the past we have put on a program for parents that simulated the activities of a typical raucous youth event (we made a special effort to invite parents who were not part of the church). Periodically sponsoring a seminar for parents on a timely topic (pop music, discipline, developmental phases, communication) can be appealing. Answering written questions about the ministry, after some reflection, can help to satisfy their need to be informed.

Other youth/denominational leaders. In my opinion, we should not get bogged down in a regional apparatus. Cooperative ventures in youth ministry can be of value—and they require considerable planning. But to take time to fill a perfunctory position that accomplishes little for the kids is not good stewardship. Sticking with our priorities will steer us away from most conflicts between our obligations at home and our dues to the district.

Schools and social service agencies. Every youth minister should develop an extensive referral system, including contacts with responsive officials in these agencies. Smooth, cordial relationships make us even more effective in our work.

The commendation of the adults in the church gives a powerful impetus to the specialized ministry God has carved out for us. Infighting can quench the brightest hopes and quickly discourage everyone involved. Without trying, youth ministry draws attention to itself in such a way that the disposition and performance of the youth leaders will be crucial. Wisdom and discernment are indispensable.

A chip on the shoulder, while not uncommon, is unbecoming. True humility, which does not pretend to know everything nor disdain supposedly "out-of-it" adults, is preferred. At the same time, directness, though always a risk, enables people to understand and count on us.

The youth minister should try to uncover the motives behind comments and criticisms—perhaps there is a hidden agenda beneath the gripe. Once we have dredged the unstated, we can resume our quest to identify shared objectives, and when we mutually affirm the ends of our ministry, the debate over means will be more fraternal.

For example, suppose a parent or board member objects to allowing first-time newcomers to sign up for the seasonal ski trip. Rather than pursuing a circular argument about the rules for registration, we might back all the way up to a disclosure of our goals for this activity. Why do we have a ski trip? What benefits do we expect? In most discussions we would come close to an agreement. Assured of our mutual good will (and theological orthodoxy), we can then reconstruct the merits of the means of selection without resorting to spurious insinuations. Factors such as the number of people wanting to go versus the number of spaces, the type of program envisioned, and past experience with newcomers on the trip have all been considered and conform with our central purpose.

The procedure for making decisions and gaining approval should be structured in a well-defined, streamlined manner. Ambiguities will be tested at a later date, possibly in the heat of conflict. Clarification of roles and responsibilities can provide early relief from endless rounds of controversy.

Every youth leader will make mistakes and should feel free to admit them. Apologies and restitution get far more accomplished than covering up missteps. Our defense is best left to those who choose to rally to our side. The youth leader who constantly whines about mistreatment will not be productive or inspire confidence.

Grateful and expeditious acknowledgment of the contributions of other adults is part of an affirmative youth ministry. Their feelings should be important to us, and we need to go out of our way to express our appreciation. Conflicts can usually be resolved with a greater dispatch when there is a reserve of good feeling.

EXCUSES

Are there churches so riddled with liabilities that youth ministry is impossible? There probably are, but often the cause of the problem is as much the intractible attitude of the youth leadership as it is the impediments of the church itself. Discouragement engenders defeat. Gloom begets doom. We are too busy excusing ourselves. No one can pretend that it will be easy, but there is always a way. There is irrefutable biblical warrant for ministering to the most unsuitable people in the most improbable places by the most unlikely means. There are appalling problems, but they can be overcome by people who care, who are trained, and who enter this impossible profession in the fortitude of the Lord.

Furthermore, it is precisely within this sort of challenging milieu that we need to launch or recover a ministry to young people. If we are looking for an effortless task, we should not consider youth work. There are plenty of other secure nine-to-five jobs available, and almost any other volunteer position in the church (from folding bulletins to chairing the trustees committee) is less clamorous.

Many times we are in danger of committing the *naturalistic fallacy* in ministry. This happens when we see a listless church or an insipid, lackluster youth ministry and conclude that this is the way it always must be. Christ Himself wants to arouse us to a sanctified opportunism that refuses to deny His leading even if it is into a hopelessly sterile or besieged setting.

Can a small church effectively minister to teenagers? Yes. Every large, thriving church was once a small one. Besides, we are not ordered to engineer miraculous results but to faithfully serve the One who routinely dispenses miracles. We can build from the ground up. We must remember that there are a lot of young people out there and that the megachurch down the street with the world-famous youth program is barely making a dent into their subculture.

I suppose a rural church that reached every teenager within a fifty-mile radius can close its books—temporarily. The rest of us are still on the hook. Starting small, incidentally, can be to our advantage. There is very little tradition to revere, few expectations (no one thinks it can be done anyway), and little pressure. We can start at a personal level and build, without undue interference, according to the convictions of our philosophy.

What about the moderate-size but lifeless church? Can it be revived? Of course, but that is primarily God's problem. It is up to us to manifest liveliness and not sit in arrogant judgment of others. Think how significant any improvement will be; any new signs of life will be greatly appreciated.

Spirituality is not introduced by gimmicks. We need to return to our foundation, to reestablish ourselves in the Source of all life, and to allow the lifeblood to flow from the inside out.

Some churches limit youth ministry by the quirky restrictions they impose on the program. Is death by strangulation inevitable? Every church, in some way, will be limiting. But there is always a way under, over, around, or through the roadblocks. Sometimes we have to work within limits to which we vociferously object; it is surprising how much we can live without while still continuing to lobby for reform. Unless we are completely shut down by the church authorities and no longer free to pursue our basic approach to ministry, we should carry on despite the handicaps.

When does a youth leader quit? The vast majority leave too soon and without adequate justification. There is no ideal church. Some form of institutional strife exists everywhere.

It takes time to develop a full-grown incarnational ministry—it takes about two years just to get started. If we are climbing the rungs toward personal recognition and success or hopping around to escape the rising temperature, we may always be one too many steps ahead of real effectiveness and fulfillment.

We must remember that Jesus took time to build His ministry. He nurtured relationships, confronted problems realistically, discipled those closest to Him, and never hurried to accomplish His goals. We should emulate Him. He is the perfect minister, and He has called us to be like Him, to minister to others as He has ministered to us; He has called us to care.

QUESTIONS

1. Is conflict inevitable in youth ministry?

2. What would you have done if you were the author at odds with his pastor? How would you estimate your diplomatic tact? Your confrontational integrity?

3. Describe a conflict you witnessed in a youth group and how it was handled.

4. How can youth leaders minimize the need to respond to disciplinary problems? Do you think these suggestions will work?

5. How do you handle defiance? Are you satisfied with your approach?

6. Are you responsible for the kids in your youth group? What does that mean?

7. "Only those who see themselves as full-fledged adults can minister to youth effectively." Please explain.

8. What difficulties can arise between parents and youth leaders? How can they be resolved?

9. What excuses do you make for those aspects of your ministry that are less effective than they could be? Is there an answer for each excuse?

10. When would you quit? How determined are you to see this ministry through? What do you need in order to carry on?

APPENDIX A

PERIODICALS OF INTEREST TO YOUTH WORKERS

Campus Life (magazine)
Box 2720
Boulder, CO 80322

Character II
P.O. Box 1149
Wheaton, IL 60189

Christian Athlete (magazine)
Fellowship of Christian Athletes
8701 Leeds Road
Kansas City, MO 64129

Christian Education Trends (newsletter)
David C. Cook Pub. Co.
Elgin, IL 60120

Christianity Today (magazine)
465 Gundersen Drive
Carol Stream, IL 60187

Contemporary Christian (magazine)
CCM Publications, Inc.
P.O. Box 6300
Laguna Hills, CA 92653

Discipleship (journal)
The Navigators
P.O. 1113
Dover, NJ 07801

Eternity (magazine)
1716 Spruce Street
Philadelphia, PA 19103

Group (Leaders' Edition) (magazine)
P.O. Box 202
Mount Morris, IL 61054

Innovations (magazine)
100 Leadership Lane
P.O. Box 1945
Marion, OH 43306

HIS (magazine)
5206 Main Street
Downers Grove, IL 60515

Journal of Christian Education
Scripture Press
P.O. Box 513
Glen Ellyn, IL

Journal of Youth and Adolescence
Plenum Publishing Corp.
233 Spring Street
New York, NY 10013

Leadership (journal)
P.O. Box 1105
Dover, NJ 07801

NEA Today (newspaper)
National Education Association
1201 16th Street, NW
Washington, DC 20036

Newsweek/Time/U.S. News & World Report
(weekly news magazines)

Parables (letter)
Saratoga Press
14200 Victor Place
Saratoga, CA 95070

Resources for Youth Ministry
Board for Youth Services
1333 South Kirkwood Road
St. Louis, MO 63122-7295

Rolling Stone (magazine)
Straight Arrow Publishers
745 Fifth Avenue
New York, NY 10151

Sojourners (magazine)
1309 L. Street, NW
Washington, DC 20005

Sources & Resources (newsletter)
Youth Specialties
1224 Greenfield Drive
El Cajon, CA 92021

Spiritual Counterfeits Project Newsletter
P.O. Box 4308
Berkeley, CA 92021

The Wittenburg Door (magazine)
Youth Specialties
1224 Greenfield Drive
El Cajon, CA 92021

Youthletter (newsletter)
Evangelical Ministries, Inc.
1716 Spruce Street
Philadelphia, PA 19103

Youthworker (journal)
Youth Specialties
1224 Greenfield Drive
El Cajon, CA 92021

APPENDIX B

A SELECTION OF POPULAR MEDIA FEATURING ADOLESCENTS
AND THEIR WORLD

FILMS

All the Right Moves
American Graffiti
Angel Dusted
Animal House
Another State of Mind
Bad Boys
Best Little Girl
Blackboard Jungle, The
Blue Lagoon
Breakfast Club, The
Breakin'
Breaking Away
Buddy Holly Story, The
Carrie
Christianne F.
Clockwork Orange, A
Coach of the Year
Cooley High
Crisis at Central High
Cross and the Switchblade, The
Dawn
Death Be Not Proud
Diary of Anne Frank, The
Easy Rider
Eddie and the Cruisers
Epidemic
Fallen Angel
Fame
Fast Times at Ridgemont High
Flaming Kid, The
Footloose
Forever
Foxes
Freaky Friday

Freedom
Getting Straight
Go Ask Alice
Goodbye Columbus
Graduate, The
Great Santini, The
Grease
Gregory's Girl
Growing Up Stoned
Hardcore
Hero Ain't Nothin' But a Sand-
    wich, A
Heros of Rock and Roll
High School, U.S.A.
Impossible Years, The
I Never Promised You a Rose
    Garden
James At Fifteen
Karate Kid
Last Picture Show, The
Liar's Moon
Little Darlings
Little Ladies of the Night
Little Romance, A
Long Way Home, A
Mask
Midnight Express
My Bodyguard
Off The Minnesota Strip
Old Enough To Do Time
One on One
Ordinary People
Other Side of the Mountain, The
Our Time
Outsiders, The

Over the Edge
Panic in Needle Park
Paper Chase
Pauline at the Beach
Please, Sir
Prime of Miss Jean Brody, The
Private Lessons
Puberty Blues
Rebel Without a Cause
Road Warrior
Rumble Fish
Running My Way
Saturday Night Fever
Scared Straight
Scarred
Secrets for Surviving
Seventeen
Silence of The Heart
Sixteen Candles
Something About Amelia
Sterile Cuckoo
Suddenly Last Summer
Summer of '42
Surviving
Taking Off
Taps
Teachers
Tex
This Is Spinal Tap
Ticket to Heaven
Times Square
To Sir With Love
Up the Down Staircase
Valley Girl
Vision Quest
War Games
Warriors, The
Westside Story
Wild in the Streets
Woodstock

TELEVISION SHOWS
(ARRANGED
CHRONOLOGICALLY)

My Three Sons ('60s)
Room 222 (late '60s, early '70s)
Lucas Tanner (early '70s)
Paper Chase (mid '70s, early '80s)
Family (mid to late '70s)
Waltons, The (mid to late '70s)
Eight Is Enough (mid to late '70s)
White Shadow (late '70s, early '80s)
Righteous Apples (late '70s, early '80s)
Facts of Life (late '70s to mid '80s)
Different Strokes (late '70s to mid '80s)
Fame (early '80s)
Making the Grade (early '80s)
Teachers Only (early '80s)
Square Pegs (early '80s)
Family Tree (early '80s)
It Takes Two (early '80s)
Family Ties (early '80s)
Why in the World (early '80s)
CBS Schoolbreak Specials (early '80s)
Boone (early '80s)
Two Marriages (early '80s)
Silver Spoons (early to mid '80s)
MTV (early to mid '80s)
Punky Brewster (mid '80s)
Who's The Boss (mid '80s)
Spencer (mid '80s)
Two Marriages (mid '80s)
Bill Cosby Show, The (mid '80s)

APPENDIX C

NATIONAL YOUTH MINISTRIES RESOURCE ORGANIZATIONS
AND SERVICES

Abingdon Publishing Co.
201 Eighth Ave.
Nashville, TN 37202

Accelerated Christian Education
P.O. Box 1438
Lewisville, TX 75067

Agape Force Resource
P.O. Box 4447
Federal Way, WA 98063

American Baptist Churches Dept. of Ministry with Youth
Valley Forge, PA 19481

Argus Communications
7440 Natchez Ave.
Niles, IL 60648

Azusa-Pacific College Dept. of Ministry
Azusa, CA 91702

Baptist General Conference Board of Christian Education
1233 Central St.
Evanston, IL 60201

Bethel Theological Seminary Youth Ministries Program
St. Paul, MN 55112

Board for Youth Services
1333 South Kirkwood Road
St. Louis, MO 63122-7295

Bread For The World
32 Union Square East
New York, NY 10003

CAMFEL Productions
136 West Olive Ave.
Monrovia, CA 91016

Campus Crusade For Christ, International
Arrowhead Springs
San Bernardino, CA 92414

High School Ministries (Student Venture)
9948 Hibart St., Suite 200
San Diego, CA 92131

Campus Life
P.O. Box 1149
Wheaton, IL 60189

The Center For Early Adolescence
Suite 223, Carr Mill Mall
Carrboro, NC 27510

C-4 Resources
Box 1408
Champagne, IL 61820

Christian Action Council
422 C St., NE
Washington, D.C. 20002

Christian Camping International
Box 646
Wheaton, IL 60187

Christian Endeavor
Box 1110
Columbus, OH 43216

Christian College Coalition
1776 Massachusetts Ave., NW
Washington, DC 20036

Christians for Urban Justice
563A Washington St.
Dorchester, MA 02124

Christians Service Brigade
Box 150
Wheaton, IL 60187

Church Youth Development
P.O. Box 652
Brentwood, TN 37027

Compassion International
P.O. Box 7000
Colorado Springs, CO 80933

Cornerstone Ministries
P.O. Box 615
Bass Lake, CA 93604

Covenant Players
Box 697
Reseda, CA 91335

Creative Youth Ministry Models
500 Common St.
Shreveport, LA 71101

Dallas Theological Seminary Christian Education Department
3909 Swiss Ave.
Dallas, TX 75204

David C. Cook, Pub.
850 North Grove Ave.
Elgin, IL 60120

Eastern College Youth Ministry Major
St. Davids, PA 19087

Eerdmans Publishing Co.
255 Jefferson Ave., SE
Grand Rapids, MI 49503

Evangelicals for Social Action
P.O. Box 76560
Washington, D.C. 20013

Evangelical Ministries
1716 Spruce St.
Philadelphia, PA 19103

Family Films
14622 Lanark St.
Panorama City, CA 91402

Fellowship of Christian Athletes
8701 Leeds Rd.
Kansas City, MO 64129

Focus On The Family
41 E. Foothill Blvd.
Arcadia, CA 91006

Food For The Hungry
7729 E. Greenway Road
Scottsdale, AZ 85260

Fuller Theological Seminary Institute of Youth Ministry
134 North Oakland Ave.
Pasadena, CA 91101

Gateway Films
P.O. Box A
Lansdale, PA 19466

Gordon-Conwell Theological Seminary Department of Youth Ministry
South Hamilton, MA 01982

Gospel Films
Box 455
Muskegon, MI 49443

Harper & Row Publishers
1700 Montgomery St.
San Francisco, CA 94111

Gospel Light Pub., International Center for Learning
Box 1650
Glendale, CA 91209

Harvest House Pub.
1075 Arrowsmith
Eugene, OR 97402

Heavy Light Productions
R3 Dept. 8
Howe, IN 46746

InterVarsity Christian Fellowship
233 Langdon St.
Madison, WI 53703

InterVarsity Press
Downers Grove, IL 60515

Institute in Basic Youth Conflicts
Box 1
Oak Brook, IL 60521

Jews For Jesus
60 Haight St.
San Francisco, CA 94102

John Knox Press
Dept. YS
P.O. Box 54658
Atlanta, GA 30308

Lamb's Players
500 E. Plaza Blvd.
National City, CA 92050

The Lutheran Church in America
2900 Queen Lane
Philadelphia, PA 19129

Lutheran Youth Encounter
2500 39th Ave., NE
Minneapolis, MN 55421

Mass Media Ministries
2116 North Charles St.
Baltimore, MD 21218

National Association of Christian Singles
P.O. Box 11394
Kansas City, MO 49510

National Association of Evangelicals
1430 K St., NW Suite 900
Washington, D.C. 20005

National Catholic Youth Organization Federation
1312 Massachusetts Ave., NW
Washington, D.C. 20005

National Network of Youth Ministries
P.O. Box 26146
San Diego, CA 92126

The Navigators
P.O. Box 20
Colorado Springs, CO 80901

Nido Qubein & Assoc.
P.O. Box 5367
High Point, NC 27262

Northeast Center for Youth Ministries
869 Broadway
Paterson, NJ 07514

O.C. Ministries
P.O. Box 66
Santa Clara, CA 95052

Omega Films
428 Eighth St.
Del Mar, CA 92014

Outreach Films
Box 4029
Westlake Village, CA 91359

Paragon Productions
Arrowhead Springs
San Bernardino, CA 92414

Paulist Productions
P.O. Box 1057
Pacific Palisades, CA 90272

Pioneer Clubs
Box 788
Wheaton, IL 06187

Prison Fellowship
P.O. Box 40562
Washington, DC 20016

Pyramid Films
P.O. Box 1048
Santa Monica, CA 90406

Reach Out Ministries
3117 Majestic Circle
Avondale Estates, GA 30002

Scripture Press
Sonpower Youth Sources
1825 College Ave.
Wheaton, IL 60187

Serendipity House
Box 7661
Colorado Springs, CO 80933

Shepherd Productions
P.O. Box 512
Englewood, CO 80151

Songs and Creations
P.O. Box 7
San Anselmo, CA 94960

Sonlife
Moody Bible Institute
820 La Salle Dr.
Chicago, IL 60610

Spiritual Counterfeits Project
P.O. Box 4308
Berkeley, CA 94604

Standard Publishing
8121 Hamilton Ave.
Cincinnati, OH 45231

Street Level Artists Agency
38 Raymond Ave., Suite 8
Pasadena, CA 91105

Success With Youth
P.O. Box 27028
Tempe, AZ 85282

Summit Expeditions
P.O. Box 521
San Dimas, CA 91773

Teen Challenge
444 Clinton Ave.
Brooklyn, NY 11238

Teen Missions
628 S. Barranca
Covina, CA 91723

TeleKetics
1229 So. Santee St.
Los Angeles, CA 90015

Thomas Schultz Pub.
P.O. Box 481
Loveland, CO 80539

The Train Depot
982 El Monte Ave.
Mountain View, CA 94040

United Methodist Church Board of Discipleship
P.O. Box 840
Nashville, TN 37202

United States Catholic Conference
National Catholic Youth Org.
Dept. of Education
1312 Massachusetts Ave., NW
Washington, DC 20005

Voice of Calvary
P.O. Box 10562
Jackson, MS 39209

Western Conservative Baptist Seminary Christian Education Program
5511 SE Hawthorne Blvd.
Portland, OR 97215

Wheaton College Graduate School
Christian Ministry Program; Center for Learning
Wheaton, IL 60187

Word of Life
Schroon Lake, NY 12870

Word Marketing Service
Box 1790
Waco, TX 76795

World Concern
Box 33000
Seattle, WA 98133

World Relief
P.O. Box WRC
Wheaton, IL 60187

World Vision
Box O
Pasadena, CA 91109

World Wide Pictures
1201 Hennepin Ave.
Minneapolis, MN 55472

Young Calvinist Federation, Reformed Church
P.O. Box 7244
Grand Rapids, MI 49510

Young Life International Service Center
P.O. Box 520
Colorado Springs, CO 80901

Youth Life Urban Ministry
5903 W. Fulton
Chicago, IL 60644

Youth Alive
Youth Dept.
1445 Boonville
Springfield, MO 65802

Youth For Christ International/Youth Guidance
P.O. Box 419
Wheaton, IL 60187

Youthleader Resource Deck
202 S. Fifth St.
Goshen, IN 46526

Youth Leadership
122 W. Franklin Ave.
Minneapolis, MN 55404

Youth Specialties Ministries
1224 Greenfield Dr.
El Cajon, CA 92021

Youth With A Mission
P.O. Box 4600
Tyler, TX 75712

Zondervan Publishing Co.
1415 Lake Drive, SE
Grand Rapids, MI 49506

NOTES

CHAPTER 1

1. Lawrence O. Richards, *Youth Ministry* (Grand Rapids, Mich.: Zondervan, 1979), 25.
2. John R.W. Stott, *Christian Counter-Culture* (Downers Grove, Ill.: InterVarsity Press, 1978), 65.
3. Rebecca Manley Pippert, *Out of the Salt Shaker* (Downers Grove, Ill.: InterVarsity Press, 1979), 11–12.
4. Jamie Buckingham, "Please Don't Call Me Reverend," *Charisma,* June 1981, 10.
5. Addresses by Jerry Kaufman, Barrington College Convocation Series, Barrington, R.I., February 1982.
6. Gerhard Kittel, ed., *Theological Dictionary of the New Testament,* vol. 2, translated by Geoffrey W. Bromiley, s.v. *diakonos,* by Hermann Beyer, (Grand Rapids, Mich.: Eerdmans Pub. Co., 1965), 88–93.

CHAPTER 2

1. Mark Patinkin, "Sweet Sixteens Leave Him Feeling Sour," *Providence Evening Bulletin,* 21 January 1982.
2. Stephen P. Morin, "For Lisa, The Justice System Made Things Worse," *Providence Sunday Journal,* 21 February 1982.
3. Nickie McWhorter, "The Subtle Kind of Child Abuse That 'Decent People' Practice," *San Francisco Sunday Examiner and Chronicle,* 10 June 1979, 6 (Scene).
4. Arthur T. Jersild, Judith S. Brook, and David W. Brook, *The Psychology of Adolescence,* 3rd ed. (New York: Macmillan, 1978), 148–156.
5. Erik Erikson, *Identity: Youth and Crisis* (New York: W.W. Norton and Co., 1968), 128–138.
6. James Marcia, "Identity In Adolescence," in *Handbook of Adolescent Psychology,* ed. Joseph Adelson (New York: John Wiley and Sons, 1980), 159–181.
7. Thomas C. Hennessy, ed., *Values and Moral Development* (New York: Paulist Press, 1976), 2–8.
8. "Suicide Among Young Surges: Drug Abuse, Divorce Are Cited," *Chicago Tribune,* May 1981.
9. Mary Ann O'Roark, "Teenage Suicide," *McCall's,* January 1982, 14, 16, 22, 120.
10. *Changing Times,* June 1982, 27–28.

11. "A Pregnant Teenager Says Goodby and Dies Beneath a Train in Md.," *Providence Journal*, March 1983.

CHAPTER 3

1. James W. Sire, "The Newest Intellectual Fashion," *Eternity*, November 1975, 40–41.
2. "End of the Permissive Society?" *U.S. News & World Report*, 28 June 1982, 45–48.
3. "Flaunting Wealth," *U.S. News & World Report*, 21 September 1981, 61–64.
4. William Pannell, "Somewhat Short of the Second Coming," *Sojourners*, September 1981, 20–21.
5. Christopher Lasch, *Culture of Narcissism* (New York: Warner, 1979).
6. Abstract of article from *Adolescence*, as quoted in *Christian Education Trends*, ed. Joseph Bayly, 10 December 1980.
7. "Troubled Teenagers," *U.S. News & World Report*, 14 December 1981, 40–43.
8. Christopher Johnson, "Subcultures in the High Schools," *Today's Education*, April–May 1981, 30–32.
9. Ralph Keyes, *Is There Life After High School?* (New York: Warner Books, 1976).
10. Don Reese with John Underwood, "I'm Not Worth a Damn," *Sports Illustrated*, 14 June 1982, 66–79.
11. Letter from Newman Pickering to the editor of *Sports Illustrated*, 28 June 1982, 84–85.
12. *Providence Journal*, March 1983.
13. Survey conducted for the National Institute on Alcohol and Alcoholism by the Research Triangle Institute (North Carolina), quoted in *Sources & Resources* (Youth Specialties), 1981.
14. William Eck (Penn. State Univ.), quoted in *Youthletter*, February 1982, 10.
15. *Youthletter*, April 1983, 2.
16. Report by the World Health Organization, noted in "New Report on the Risks of Pot," *Providence Journal*, April 1982.
17. "Crashing on Cocaine," *Time*, 11 April 1983, 22–31.
18. National Institute of Drug Abuse, cited in "Cocaine-Related Deaths Rising Sharply," *Providence Journal*, May 1982, 2.
19. Robert Lindsey and Aljean Harmetz, "An Epidemic of Drugs Hits Hollywood as Old Taboos Fall," *Providence Journal*, 7 November 1982, B1, B10.
20. Weldon L. Witters and Patricia Jones-Witters, *Drugs and Sex*, (New York: Macmillan, 1975), 120.

21. Joseph A. Califano, Jr., *Drug Abuse and Alcoholism* (New York: Warner Books, 1982), 51.
22. "Look Alikes: A New Drug Danger," *Time*, 21 September 1981, 69.
23. "Great American Smokeout Is Today," *Boston Globe*, 18 November 1982, 20.
24. Nicholas Pileggi, "Drug Business," *New York*, 13 December 1982, 38–43.
25. Mary Fortney, "Teenage Sex," *Redwood City Tribune*, 28 November 1977, 1, 5.
26. Sally Bedell, "A Critical Look at TV's Distorted Image of Adolescents," *TV Guide*, 4 July 1981, 5–8.
27. "At Sixteen, Seventeen . . ." *San Francisco Chronicle*, 13 May 1979, 34.
28. *Youthletter*, November 1981, 82–83.
29. Tony Lioce, "Why Is This Man Snarling?" *Providence Journal Bulletin*, 26 March 1983.
30. Quoted from Tom Cottle, *Providence Journal*, February 1981.
31. *Today's Education*, Nov.–Dec. 1981, 25ff.
32. Michael Janusonis, "Movies Aimed at Kids Fail to Reflect What Life Is Like for Young People," *Providence Journal Bulletin*, 19, I11.
33. Report by National Commission on Excellence in Education, in "U.S. Schools Are Failing," *Providence Journal*, 26 April 1983, A1, A4.
34. Mary Ann Seawell, "No One Is Immune, Cult Victim Warns," *Peninsula Times Tribune* (San Francisco Peninsula), 24 May 1979, C6.

CHAPTER 4

1. H. Richard Niebuhr, *Christ and Culture* (New York: Harper & Row, 1975), 39–44ff.
2. Robert Palmer, "Rock: No Longer 'The Devil's Music'?" *New York Times*, 16 September 1981.
3. Charles Colson, "Religion Up, Morality Down," n.p.
4. Joe Byly, "Walking Parables," *Eternity*, September 1981.
5. Stan Mooneyham, "Faithfulness and the Present Tense," *World Vision*, April 1981, 23.
6. From the text of remarks made by Alexander Solzhenitsyn, pub. in Stanford University *Campus Report*, 2 June 1976.

CHAPTER 5

1. Text from Oscar Romero's speech given in Belgium in February 1980, translated in "Taking Risks for the Poor," in *World Vision,* April 1982, 6–7.
2. Ian Thomas (unattributed source).
3. Stan Mooneyham, "Let's All Rise from Our Seats," *World Vision,* July 1980, 23.
4. Richard Halverson, "How I Changed My Thinking About the Church," *Eternity,* October 1975, 37–38.
5. Joseph Aldrich, "You Are a Message," *Moody Monthly,* 1982.

CHAPTER 6

1. Dietrich Bonhoeffer, *Life Together* (New York: Harper & Row, 1954), 31–37.
2. Stan Mooneyham, "Souls Are For More Than Winning," *World Vision,* April 1982, 23.
3. Richard John Neuhaus, quoted in "Do You Have That Jesus Glitter?" *Sources & Resources,* 15 June 1981.
4. C.S. Lewis, *The Great Divorce* (New York: Macmillan, 1946).

CHAPTER 8

1. Rickey Short, "The Youth Minister's First Crisis," *Leadership,* Spring 1982, 83–87.

BIBLIOGRAPHY

THEOLOGICAL ORIENTATION TO MINISTRY

Anderson, Ray, ed. *Theological Foundations for Ministry.* Grand Rapids, Mich.: Eerdmans Pub. Co., 1979.
Bright, John. *The Kingdom of God.* Nashville: Abingdon Press, 1953.
Colson, Charles. *Loving God.* Grand Rapids: Zondervan, 1983.
Heschel, Abraham. *The Prophets.* 2 vols. New York: Harper & Row, 1971.
Mooneyham, Stan. "The Heresy of Half-Truth." *World Vision,* June 1982.
Niebuhr, H. Richard. *Christ and Culture.* New York: Harper & Row, 1975.
Palmer, Earl F. *The Intimate Gospel.* Waco, Tex.: Word Books, 1978.
Sine, Tom. *The Mustard Seed Conspiracy.* Waco, Tex.: Word Books, 1981.
Smedes, Lewis B. *Love Within Limits.* Grand Rapids, Mich.: Eerdmans Pub. Co., 1980.
Stott, John R.W. *Christian Counter-Culture.* Downers Grove, Ill.: InterVarsity Press, 1978.
Stott, John R.W., and Robert Coote. *Down to Earth.* Grand Rapids, Mich.: Eerdmans Pub. Co., 1980.
Thielicke, Helmut. *I Believe.* Philadelphia: Fortress Press, 1979.
Wallis, Jim. *The Call to Conversion.* New York: Harper & Row, 1982.

ECCLESIOLOGY

Bonhoeffer, Dietrich. *Life Together.* New York: Harper & Row, 1954.
Buzzard, Lynn R., and Samuel Ericsson. *The Battle for Religious Liberty.* Elgin, Ill.: David C. Cook Pub. Co., 1982.
Kung, Hans. *The Church.* Garden City, N.Y.: Image Books, 1976.
McGavran, Donald A. *How Churches Grow.* New York: Friendship Press, 1970.
Raines, Robert A. *New Life in the Church.* New York: Harper & Row, 1961.
Slosser, Bob. *Miracle in Darien.* Plainfield, N.J.: Logos, Int., 1979.
Snyder, Howard A. *Liberating the Church.* Downers Grove, Ill.: InterVarsity Press, 1983.
Snyder, Howard A. *Wineskins.* Downers Grove, Ill.: InterVarsity Press, 1976.
Stedman, Ray C. *Body Life.* Glendale, Calif.: Gospel Light Publications, 1972.

Tillapaugh, Frank. *The Church Unleashed.* Ventura, Calif.: Regal Books, 1982.

ISSUES IN LEADERSHIP AND DISCIPLESHIP

Ahlem, Lloyd H. "Deference." *Covenant Companion,* January 1980.

Ahlem, Lloyd H. "Sanctified Neurosis." *Covenant Companion,* September 1980.

Christian, S. Rickley. *Alive!* Grand Rapids, Mich.: Zondervan; Wheaton, Ill.: Campus Life, 1983.

Coleman, Robert E. *The Master Plan of Evangelism.* Old Tappan, N.J.: Fleming H. Revell Co., 1969.

Eims, Leroy. *The Lost Art of Disciple Making.* Grand Rapids, Mich.: Zondervan; Colorado Springs, Colo.: Navpress, 1980.

Foster, Richard J. *Celebration of Discipline.* New York: Harper & Row, 1978.

Hanks, Billie, Jr., and William A. Shell. *Discipleship.* Grand Rapids, Mich.: Zondervan, 1981.

Hansel, Tim. *When I Relax I Feel Guilty.* Elgin, Ill.: David C. Cook Pub. Co., 1979.

Henrichsen, Walter A. *Disciples Are Made—Not Born.* Wheaton, Ill.: Victor Books, 1980.

Hyde, Douglas. *Dedication and Leadership.* Notre Dame, Ind.: University of Notre Dame Press, 1971.

Mooneyham, Stan. "God's Will—Good, Better, Best?" *World Vision,* December 1981.

Mooneyham, Stan. "If He Asks for a Scorpion." *World Vision,* July 1982.

Ortiz, Juan Carlos. *Disciple.* Carol Stream, Ill.: Creation House, 1980.

Peters, Thomas J., and Robert J. Waterman. *In Search of Excellence.* New York: Harper & Row, 1982.

Richard, Lawrence O., and Clyde Hoeldtke. *A Theology of Church Leadership.* Grand Rapids, Mich.: Zondervan, 1980.

Swindoll, Charles R. *Hand Me Another Brick.* Nashville, Tenn.: Thomas Nelson Publishers, 1978.

Tozer, A.W. "The Blessedness of Possessing Nothing." *Leadership,* Spring 1982.

Training Manual. Gordon-Conwell Theological Seminary/Young Life Youth Ministries Program, n.d.

PRINCIPLES OF RELATIONSHIP AND COMMUNICATION

Bayard, Robert T., and Jean Bayard. *How to Deal with Your Acting-Up Teenager.* New York: M. Evans and Co., 1983.

Campbell, Ross. *How To Really Love Your Teenager.* , Wheaton, Ill.: Victor Books, 1981.

Dirkmeyer, Don, and Gary D. McKay. *Systematic Training For Effective Parenting Of Teens (Parents Guide).* Circle Pines, Mich.: American Guidance Service, 1983

Ginott, Haim. *Between Parent and Teenager.* New York: Avon Books, 1971.

Glasser, William. *Reality Therapy.* New York: Harper & Row, 1975.

Griffin, Em. *Getting Together.* Downers Grove, Ill.: InterVarsity Press, 1982.

Griffin, Em. *The Mind Changers.* Wheaton, Ill.: Tyndale House, 1977.

Johnson, David W. *Reaching Out.* Englewood Cliffs, N.J.: Prentice-Hall, 1972.

Kesler, Jay with Tim Stafford. *Breakthrough.* Grand Rapids, Mich.: Zondervan; Wheaton, Ill.: Campus Life Books, 1981.

Lewis, C.S. *The Four Loves.* New York: Harbrace, 1971.

Little, Paul E. *How To Give Away Your Faith.* Downers Grove, Ill.: InterVarsity Press, 1966.

Morrow, Lance. "If Slang Is Not a Sin." *Time,* 8 November, 1982.

Pippert, Rebecca M. *Out of the Salt Shaker.* Downers Grove, Ill.: InterVarsity Press, 1979.

Powell, John. *The Secret of Staying in Love.* Niles, Ill.: Argus Communications, 1974.

Powell, John. *Why Am I Afraid to Tell You Who I Am?* Niles, Ill.: Argus Communications, 1974.

Richardson, Jerry, and Joel Margulis. *The Magic of Rapport.* San Francisco: Harbor Pub., 1981.

Shostrom, Everett L. *Man, the Manipulator.* Nashville: Bantam Books, 1979.

Stafford, Tim. *A Love Story.* Grand Rapids, Mich.: Zondervan; Wheaton, Ill.: Campus Life Books, 1981.

Stott, John R.W. *Between Two Worlds.* Grand Rapids, Mich.: Eerdmans Pub. Co., 1982.

Tournier, Paul. *The Meaning of Persons.* New York: Harper & Row, 1957.

Trobisch, Walter. *I Loved a Girl.* New York: Harper & Row, 1965.

Witte, Kaaren. *Angels in Faded Jeans.* Minneapolis: Jeremy Books, 1979.

Yancey, Philip. *Where is God When It Hurts?* Grand Rapids, Mich.: Zondervan; Wheaton, Ill.: Campus Life Books, 1977.

YOUTH MINISTRY STRATEGIES

Borthwick, Paul. "How to Keep a Youth Minister." *Leadership,* Winter 1983.

Coleman, Bill, and Patty Coleman. *Parish Youth Ministry.* Mystic, Conn.: Twenty-Third Pub., 1977.

Cousins, Don. *Son City.* Elk Grove Village, Ill.: Kukla Press, 1979.

Dunphy-Linnartz, Bernie C. *Strategies for Youth Programs.* vol. 3 n.p.: Geneva Press, 1980.

Flood, Robert. "Who's Helping the Youth Pastor?" *Moody Monthly,* October 1980.

Holderness, Ginny Ward. *The Exuberant Years.* Atlanta: John Knox Press, 1976.

Ludwig, Glenn E. *Building an Effective Youth Ministry.* Creative Leadership Series, ed. by Lyle E. Schaller. Nashville: Abingdon, 1980.

Martinson, Roland. "Courage, Creativity and Excellence in Youth Ministry." *Group,* June–August 1982.

Rice, Wayne. *Junior High Ministry.* Grand Rapids, Mich.: Zondervan, 1978.

Richards, Lawrence O. *Youth Ministry.* Grand Rapids, Mich.: Zondervan, 1979.

Roadcup, David, ed. *Ministering to Youth.* Cincinnati: Standard Pub., 1980.

Spader, Dann. *Sonlife Strategy of Youth Discipleship and Evangelism.* Chicago: Moody Bible Institute, 1981.

Stone, J. David. *The Complete Youth Ministries Handbook.* 2 vols. Nashville: Abingdon, 1979, 1981.

Warren, Michael. *Youth and the Future of the Church.* New York: Seabury Press, 1982.

Whittemore, Hank. "One Family Conquers Gang War." *Parade,* 4 May 1980.

Willey, Ray, ed. *Working With Youth.* Wheaton, Ill.: Victor Books, 1982.

YOUTH MINISTRIES PROGRAM RESOURCES

Alexander, John W. *Managing Our Work.* Downers Grove, Ill.: InterVarsity Press, 1978.

Anderson, Yohann, ed. *Songs.* San Anselmo, Calif.: Songs and Creations, Inc., 1983.

Barton, Bruce, ed. *Whole Person Survival Kits.* Wheaton, Ill.: Youth For Christ Int., 1976.

Benson, Dennis C., and Bill Wolfe. *The Basic Encyclopedia for Youth Ministry.* Loveland, Colo.: Group Books, 1981.

Campolo, Anthony. *Ideas For Social Action*. Edited by Wayne Rice. Grand Rapids, Mich.: Zondervan/Youth Specialties, 1983

Coleman, Lyman. *The Encyclopedia of Serendipity*. Littleton, Colo.: Serendipity House, 1980.

Coleman, Lyman. *Youth Ministry Encyclopedia*. Littleton, Colo. Serendipity House, 1984.

The Encyclopedia of Icebreakers. San Diego: University Associates, Inc., 1984.

Fluegelman, Andrew, ed. *The New Games Book*. Garden City, N.Y.: Dolphin Books, 1976.

Fluegelman, Andrew. *More New Games,* Garden City, N.Y.: Doubleday and Co., 1981.

Howard, Robert, ed. *Respond*. 5 vols. Valley Forge: Judson Press, 1977.

Klein, Chuck. *So You Want to Lead Students*. Wheaton, Ill.: Tyndale House, 1982.

Merrill, Dean and Marshall Shelley. *Fresh Ideas for Families, Youth and Children*. Waco: Word, 1984.

Miller, Chuck. *Now That I'm a Christian*. 2 vols. Glendale, Calif.: Regal Books, 1976.

Resource Directory for Youth Workers. El Cajon, Calif.: Youth Specialties Minn., 1985 (published annually).

Rice, Wayne, Danny Rydberg, and Mike Yaconelli. *Fun-N-Games*. Grand Rapids, Mich.: Zondervan, 1982.

Rice, Wayne, and Mike Yaconelli. *Ideas*. 32 vols. El Cajon, Calif.: Youth Specialties, 1968–1983.

Richards, Larry, and Norm Wakefield. *Basic Christian Values, First Steps for New and Used Christians, Fruit of the Spirit, the Good Life:* Discipling Resource Series. Grand Rapids, Mich.: Zondervan, 1981.

Skits. Colorado Springs, Colo.: Young Life National Services, n.d.

Souter, John C. *How to Grow New Christians*. Wheaton, Ill.: Tyndale House, 1979.

Sparks, Lee, ed. *The Youth Group How-To Book*. Loveland, Colo.: Group Books, 1981.

Yaconelli, Mike, and Wayne Rice. *Tension Getters*. Grand Rapids, Mich.: Zondervan. El Cajon, Calif.: Youth Specialties, 1981.

Youth Work Bibliography. St. Paul, Minn: Univ. of Minnesota (Center for Youth Development and Research), 1980.

ADOLESCENT DEVELOPMENTAL FACTORS

Adelson, Joseph. "Adolescence and the Generalization Gap." *Psychology Today,* February 1979.

Adelson, Joseph, ed. *Handbook of Adolescent Psychology.* New York: John Wiley and Sons, 1980.

Adler, Mortimer. *The Paideia Proposal.* Institute For Philosophical Research, 1982.

Billingsley, Lloyd. "Half In Love With Easeful Death." *Eternity,* March 1985.

Bruch, Hilde, *The Golden Cage.* New York: Random House, 1979.

Davitz, Joel, and Lois Davitz. "How to Live Almost Happily with a Teenager." *McCall's,* January 1981.

Erikson, Erik. *Identity: Youth and Crisis.* New York: W.W. Norton and Co., 1968.

Gallatin, Judith E. *Adolescence and Individuality.* New York: Harper & Row, Pub., 1975.

Green, Hannah. *I Never Promised You a Rose Garden.* New York: Holt, Rinehart, and Winston, 1964.

Groller, Ingrid. "Good Teens." *Parents,* June 1983.

Hennessy, Thomas C., ed. *Values and Moral Development.* New York: Paulist Press, 1976.

Jersild, Arthur T., Judith S. Brook, and David W. Brook. *The Psychology of Adolescence.* New York: Macmillan Co., 1978.

Johnson, Lissa. *Just Like Ice Cream.* Palm Springs, Calif.: Ronald N. Haynes Pub., 1982.

Kagan, Jerome, and Robert Coles, eds. *12 To 16: Early Adolescence.* New York: W.W. Norton and Co., 1972.

Kohlberg, Lawrence. *The Philosophy of Moral Development.* San Francisco: Harper & Row, Pub., 1981.

Kohn, Alfie. "Teenagers Under Glass." *Psychology Today,* July 1984.

McCoy, Kathy, and Charles Wibblesman. *The Teenage Body Book.* New York: Penguin Books, 1979.

Narramore, Bruce. *Adolescence Is Not an Illness.* Old Tappan, N.J.: Fleming H. Revell, Co., 1980.

Offer, Daniel, et al. *The Adolescent: A Psychological Self-Portrait.* New York: Basic Books, 1981.

Rogers, Dorothy. *Adolescents and Youth.* Englewood Cliffs, N.J.: Prentice-Hall, 1981.

Sprinthall, Richard, and Norman Sprinthall. *Educational Psychology: A Developmental Approach.* 3rd ed. Reading, Mass.: Addison-Wesley Pub. Co., 1981.

Stein, Michael D., and J. Kent Davis. *Therapies for Adolescents.* San Francisco: Jossey-Bass Pub., 1982.

MACROTRENDS

Bartel, Dennis. *Who's Who In Gurus*. San Francisco Examiner, 18 March, 1984.

Califano, Joseph A. *Drug Abuse and Alcoholism*. New York: Warner Books, 1982.

Crozier, Michael. "The Trouble With America."*San Francisco Examiner,* 26 August 1984.

Enroth, Ronald, et al. *A Guide to Cults and New Religions*. Downers Grove, Ill.: InterVarsity Press, 1983.

Forbes, Cheryl. *The Religion of Power*. Grand Rapids, Mich.: Zondervan, 1983.

"Global 2000 Revisited." Summary of report presented at the annual meeting of the American Association for the Advancement of Science. *Chicago Tribune,* 28 May 1983.

Lasch, Christopher. *Culture of Narcissism*. New York: Warner Books, 1979.

Leo, John. "The Revolution Is Over." *Time,* 9 April, 1984.

Leonard, George, "The End of Sex." *Esquire,* December 1982.

Maranto, Gina. "Coke: The Random Killer." *Discover,* March 1985.

Marllowe, Mike. "Khaki Wacky."*San Francisco Examiner,* 8 July 1984.

Montagu, Ashley, and Floyd Matson. *The Dehumanization Of Man*. New York: McGraw-Hill, 1983.

Morrow, Lance. "The Burnout of Almost Everyone." *Time,* 21 September 1981.

Nachman, Gerald. "When the Moviegoing Becomes The Only Reality." *San Francisco,* 10 February 1985.

Oden, Thomas. Editorial in *National Review,* 1979.

O'Flaherty, Terrence. "Who Is Being Fooled This April 1?" *San Francisco Examiner,* 1 April 1984.

Rifken, Jeremy, with Ted Howard. *The Emerging Order*. New York: Putnam, 1979.

Sire, James W. *The Universe Next Door*. Downers Grove, Ill.: InterVarsity Press, 1976.

Smith, Adam. *Powers of Mind*. New York: Random House, 1975.

Susman, Warren. *Culture as History*. New York: Panteon, 1985.

Toffler, Alvin. *The Third Wave*. New York: William Morrow and Co., 1980.

"U.S. Campaign Fails to Stem Wave of Cocaine." *San Francisco Examiner,* 19 February 1984.

Yankelovitch, Daniel. *New Rules*. New York: Random House, 1981.

CURRENTS IN THE YOUTH SUBCULTURE

Anders, Corrie. "How American Teens Feel: Report On The Mood Of American Youth" prepared by the National Association of Secondary School Principals. *San Francisco Examiner,* 1 April 1984.

Boyer, Ernest L. *High School.* New York: Harper & Row, 1983.

Clarke, Gerald. "New Lyrics for the Devil's Music." *Time,* 11 March 1985.

Coleman, James. *Adolescent Society.* New York: Free Press, 1971.

Connelly, Christopher. "Keeping the Faith." *Rolling Stone,* 14 March 1985.

Curtis, Diane. "Split Families Mean Trouble For Youths." *San Francisco Chronicle,* 23 March 1985.

Elkind, David. *All Grown Up and No Place To Go.* Reading, Mass.: Addison-Wesley Pub. Co., 1984.

Elkind, David. *The Hurried Child.* Reading, Mass.: Addison-Wesley Pub. Co., 1981.

Enroth, Ronald. *The Lure of the Cults.* Chappaqua, N.Y.: Christian Herald Books, 1979.

Gilmore, Mikal. "T-Bone Burnett's Moral Messages." *Rolling Stone,* 11 November 1982.

Go Ask Alice. New York: Avon, 1972.

Jaeger, Barbara. "Violence, Sex Flare In Rock World." *San Francisco Examiner,* 15 April 1984.

Henke, James. "Blessed Are the Peacemakers." *Rolling Stone,* 9 June 1983.

Keyes, Ralph. *Is There Life After High School?* New York: Warner Books, 1976.

Lawhead, Steve. *Rock Reconsidered.* Downers Grove, Ill.: InterVarsity Press, 1981.

Macroff, Gene. *Don't Blame the Kids.* New York: McGraw-Hill, 1981.

Miller, Jim, ed. *History of Rock and Roll.* New York: Random House, 1980.

Morch, Al. "Getting High on Heavy Metal." *San Francisco Chronicle,* 6 May 1984.

Norman, Jane, and Myron Harris. *The Private Life of the American Teenager.* New York: Rawson, Rade Pub., 1981.

North, Robert J., and Richard A. Orange. *Teenage Drinking.* New York: Macmillan, 1980.

Owen, David. *High School.* New York: Viking Press, 1981.

Palmer, Robert. "Messages in Rock To a New Culture." *San Francisco Chronicle,* 3 March 1985.

Rabkin, Brenda. *Growing Up Dead*. Nashville: Abingdon, 1979.

Rayl, Salley. "Censoring Graphic Sex and Violence on MTV." *San Francisco Chronicle*, 8 July 1984.

Reapsome, Jim. "Analysis" (re: John Lennon's life and death). *Youthletter*, March 1981.

Reinhart, Tara, and Steven Tate. "Class of '83." *Ladies' Home Journal*, June 1983.

Ross, Patricia. *Trouble in School*. New York: Avon Books, 1979.

"Schools Lambasted for Timidity." *Contra Costa Times*, 21 November 1984.

"Suicide Is Epidemic." *USA Today* editorial, 29 March 1985.

Witters, Weldon L., and Patricia Jones-Witters. *Drugs and Sex*. New York: Macmillan Pub. Co., 1975.

AUTOBIOGRAPHY

Colson, Charles W. *Life Sentence*. Old Tappan, N.J.: Fleming H. Revell, Co., 1979.

Eareckson, Joni, *A Step Further*. Grand Rapids, Mich.: Zondervan 1981.

Frank, Anne, *Diary of a Young Girl*. Garden City, N.Y.: Doubleday, 1967.

Lewis, C.S. *Surprised By Joy*. New York: Harcourt, Brace and World, 1955.

Milliken, Bill. *Tough Love*. Old Tappan, N.J.: Spire Books, 1968.

Perkins, John. *Let Justice Roll Down*. Ventura, Calif.: Regal, 1976.

Roberts, Rachel. *Raped*. Grand Rapids, Mich.: Zondervan, 1981.

Stone, Judy. "Unblinking View of Troubled Youth." *San Francisco Chronicle*, 26 August 1984.

Wright, Richard. *Black Boy*. New York: Harper & Row, Pub., 1969.